The Right Way To Select Technology

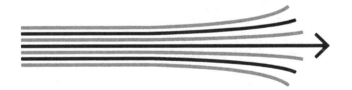

GET THE REAL STORY ON
FINDING THE BEST FIT

Digital Reality Checks is a Rosenfeld Media imprint
developed in partnership with Real Story Group.

 Rosenfeld    **Real Story** GROUP

The Right Way to Select Technology
Get the Real Story in Finding the Best Fit
By Tony Byrne and Jarrod Gingras

Rosenfeld Media, LLC

540 President Street

Brooklyn, New York

11215 USA

On the Web: www.digitalrealitychecks.com

Please send errors to: errata@rosenfeldmedia.com

Publisher: Louis Rosenfeld

Managing Editor: Marta Justak

Interior Layout: Danielle Foster

Cover Design: The Heads of State

Indexer: Joy Dean Lee

Proofreader: Sue Boshers

ISBN: 978-1-933820-54-3

ISBN-13: 978-1-933820-54-5

LCCN: 2017942114

Printed and bound in the United States of America

*Dedicated to the hundreds of enterprise leaders
who have invited us help them pick technology.*
Docendo discimus...

Who Should Read This Book?

This book is for anyone about to embark on a technology selection project, offering a practical guide to making the right decisions. We focus in particular on selecting digital workplace and marketing/engagement technologies—as these decisions will prove critical in any organization's digital transformation going forward—but our approach can be applied to selecting any kind of information technology.

The best selection decisions get made by a team, so we address the needs of a wide set of stakeholders. On the business side, this includes program and project managers, digital team leads, marketing and workplace directors, UX specialists, and program champions. On the technology side, we want to empower IT directors, architects, and developers with a practical methodology that will set them up for successful engagement with any new technologies.

In particular, we address the needs of the following people:

- Senior program or project managers who regularly select tools and want to find a better approach

- Enterprise digital leaders who want to extend proven agile methods to technology sourcing

- IT decision-makers who want to guide their selection teams more effectively

- Project business leads who may have never selected technology before and are looking for a practical guide

- The individual professional tasked with a seemingly overwhelming decision who needs a clear roadmap to engage her peers

- Enterprise procurement managers looking for best practices

- Consulting directors seeking to employ clear methodologies for selection engagements

What's in This Book?

This book is a primer on putting together the ideal selection process, based on iteration, adaptivity, and hands-on testing.

Part I, "Business Foundations," shows you how to establish solid business foundations, via a no-bullshit business case along with the right team and a clear decision-making structure.

Part II, "Needs and Opportunities," describes how to identify your *true* needs and opportunities by capturing requirements that don't suck (like they usually do), because they're based primarily on real user stories and differentiating questions.

Part III, "Conduct Market Analysis," helps you analyze market-places, to make sure you're targeting the right technology and uncovering the best set of plausible suppliers for your particular circumstances.

Part IV, "Engage with Suppliers," explains how to communicate with potential suppliers, via practical RFPs and candid Q&A sessions.

Part V, "Try Before You Buy," lays out our agile, try-before-you-buy approach, explaining how to shape meaningful demos and then find out how the tools *really* work during hands-on bake-offs.

Part VI, "Make the Right Choice," coaches you how to make the right choice, negotiating like a pro and resolving internal disagreements, as well as how to adapt this process to select professional services firms.

What Comes with This Book?

This book's companion website (**digitalrealitychecks.com/books /right-way-to-select-technology**) contains a blog and additional content. The book's diagrams and other illustrations are available under a Creative Commons license (when possible) for you to download and include in your own presentations. You can find these on Flickr at **www.flickr.com/photos/rosenfeldmedia/sets/**.

FREQUENTLY ASKED QUESTIONS

What sorts of technology are you talking about?

For the most part, we are referring to information technologies that an enterprise will procure to improve customer or employee digital experience directly or indirectly. This is a pretty broad remit, from network management software to machine learning to expense-reporting apps and much more. However, you'll find that the core methodology can be applied to selecting any information technology.

Is this book all about applying agile to technology selection?

Sort of. We don't explicitly use the term (which means many things to many people), but you'll see some universally regarded agile concepts:

- **Chapter 2**, "Build a Selection Team That Works," shows you how to build a diverse *team* of stakeholders

- **Chapters 4**, "Capture Requirements That Don't Suck," and **5**, "Why User Stories Are Everything," emphasize *story-based* narratives

- **Chapters 13** and **14** lay out an *empirical, test-based* review process

Above all, you will learn an approach that is iterative, adaptive, and *real*.

My enterprise is very old-fashioned. How can I get them to adopt this approach?

For starters, you can emphasize the business value and potential cost savings. Start with **Chapter 1**, "Craft a No-Bullshit Business Case," where we help you craft a no-bullshit business case, and end with **Chapter 15**, "Negotiate Like a Pro," by learning how to negotiate better deals on costs and terms. Show your colleagues the Introduction, which lays out everything that could go wrong with your current procurement methods. But don't forget **Chapter 16**, "Make the Right Final Selection," which explains how making a solid decision can accelerate your time to deployment.

Will this book help me select the right consultants and implementers?

Absolutely! Aligning with the right services partners—integrators, consultancies, agencies, vendor implementation teams, and more— can prove critical to your overall success. All the key concepts in the book apply to choosing services firms as well. But **Chapter 17**, "Adapt This Process for Selecting Services Firms," is totally dedicated to the topic, with specific examples of how to adapt the general methodology to the particular challenges of lining up the right outside help for implementing and supporting your technology.

How much does our choice of vendor really matter?

Potentially, quite a lot. Now, some technology consultants opine that it matters less *which* tools your enterprise deploys and more *how* you use them: the quality of the content and the data, the skills of the users, and so forth. There's some truth to that, but on the other hand, why burden your co-workers or customers with substandard digital platforms if you don't have to? Selecting the right tool is no guarantee for digital success, but it sets you up for being effective going forward. Pick the right technologies and then put your organizational assets and skills to work to exploit them.

CONTENTS

FOREWORD

I work with product teams to help them design and build more successful products. Unfortunately, I usually have bad news for them.

These teams are looking for the secret to creating great products. Like most things in life, there is no secret and there is no shortcut. Successful products don't emerge from clever feature ideas or sexy screen designs. They come from teams that understand their stakeholders, customers, and users. They come from teams that know how users work today and empathize with their challenges. They come from teams that can imagine a better way for these people to work in the future using the software and technology they're building. And they come from teams that test their ideas aggressively. Teams like this *eventually* create incredible products.

Why am I telling you all this? If you've picked up Tony and Jarrod's book, you don't plan on designing and building a product; you're looking for a technology. But it turns out that the process of selecting technology for your organization is a lot like designing it yourself. It's not going to work for you to assemble a wish list of features from within your organization and then select the vendor that says they have more of them than the next guy. You know that the best products aren't necessarily the ones with the most features. Instead, the best approach is to understand the people in your organization, their work and challenges, and imagine a better future for them using the technology you select. That's going to take some time and effort.

In this book, Tony and Jarrod lay out a straightforward way of selecting technology successfully. Brace yourself—these authors don't mince words. They directly expose the traps most organizations fall into, as well as giving straightforward ways to avoid them. This book describes a process from beginning to end in a way that even I can understand.

By working the way Tony and Jarrod suggest, you'll help your organization make one of its best investments ever. And, what's more, you'll know it when you see it, because you and your team will have already envisioned that better way to work, as well as tested it before committing. You should be proud. Well, you will be.

Oh, and the best thing is that you won't actually have to build the whole solution yourself. And that's a good thing.

—Jeff Patton
Founder, Patton & Associates
Author, *User Story Mapping*

INTRODUCTION

Industry surveys repeatedly show that more than half of technology projects fail to meet their objectives—or just fail outright.

There are many reasons for this, but in our experience, most technology problems originate in the critical early stages of an initiative. Once the boat gets headed in a particular direction, it can be hard to steer it back on course. The larger the project, the more this becomes evident.

Which vendor and technology to select for your digital initiatives becomes a critical early choice. Making the wrong pick doesn't necessarily doom a project, but it does make success much more difficult to achieve. Making the right choice doesn't guarantee your long-term success either, but starting with the right technical foundation bodes well for an enterprise fully committed to exploiting any new toolset.

What's Wrong with Traditional Selection Processes?

Unfortunately, most enterprises don't do a good job of selecting technology. We see five particular pathologies here:

- **Handy incumbent:** Picking a technology because you already license it for something else, rather than because it directly addresses the specific business goals at hand.

- **Horse race:** Picking a technology because an analyst firm or guru placed it in the top right of some inane quadrant, and not because it was a good fit for you.

- **Puppy love:** Picking a technology because you saw a demo and fell madly in love, when in fact *all* tools have serious warts under the covers.

- **Cousin Vinny:** Picking a technology because some other firm in your industry recommended it, despite the fact that your needs and profile are likely to prove quite different.

- **Checklist fetish:** Picking a technology because it passed your exhaustive spreadsheet checklist filters, which actually have little bearing on whether an interactive tool is really going to work for you.

Of all these mistakes, the fifth process is perhaps the worst, because it *feels* methodical and thorough. It assumes that you can capture all your requirements up front in one big, abstract, analytical effort and then make a decision based on mapping vendor features to your list.

In IT terms, this totally represents a "waterfall" methodology, and it suffers from all the drawbacks inherent to that approach:

- Inadequate testing and adaptation
- Inability to course-correct based on learning
- Overanalysis and underexperimentation
- Less control over schedules and outcomes
- Emphasis on "big bang" decision-making

We decided to write this book after seeing too many enterprises struggle with waterfall-based technology selection processes. At Real Story Group, we've advised hundreds of enterprises over nearly two decades to make good technology choices, and this book represents a distillation of lessons learned.

How to Do It Right

In particular, we outline a user-centered, agile-like process that not only gets you to the "best-fit" solution for your organization, but also bodes well for successful piloting and rollout of the winning technology.

Here's a quick summary of what you'll learn:

1. How to build the right foundations for a successful technology selection, with a solid team and a refreshingly no-bullshit business case.

2. How to capture and communicate requirements in ways that are truly differentiating and represent real business impact.

3. How to make sure that you're looking at the right marketplace and the best-fitting vendors for your environment.

4. How to interact with potential suppliers, including a straightforward and focused RFP or tender.

5. How to test out the solutions in competitive environments, with demos targeted to your specific needs, and hands-on bake-offs where you can try out the goods before you buy.

6. How to make the right choices throughout the process, to get to an optimal solution and set the team up for success going forward.

So think of this as a kind of cookbook, but you'll see along the way that we'll encourage you to vary the recipes, based on the scope and nature of the technology you're selecting. The appendix includes links to sample artifacts and useful video instructions.

Best wishes for starting out your digital journeys on the right path!

PART I

Business Foundations

It's an old adage in the tech world: if you don't have a solid business rationale for what you're doing, you will never achieve business value. Everyone knows this, yet many enterprises still chase technology for its own sake, selecting tools and then only later figuring out what to do with them.

The inevitable result is "shelfware"—technology awaiting deployment as real users figure out how to exploit what their employer purchased hastily. Selecting technology that explicitly addresses business priorities leads to faster time-to-value.

Digital technology initiatives frequently span across multiple departments in an organization, each holding different stakes and interests. To work toward a common purpose, you need a broadly representative governance structure that boasts both strong internal leadership as well as executive support. The time to establish this foundation is *before* you select the technology.

Finally, you need to make sure that you are ready to fully realize the benefits of any new technologies you procure. In many cases, customers are not ready, and their new systems fall prey to the same dysfunctions as their old environments. Benchmarking can help you baseline your true capacity, so you can figure out where you need to improve and perhaps reconsider the complexity of any new tooling you pursue.

This section will lead you through an approach to ensuring that solid business foundations and processes underpin your technology selection and deployment.

- Chapter 1, "Craft a No-Bullshit Business Case," will show you different approaches to articulating a realistic business case and offer a primer on how to approach the long-term, total cost of ownership.

- Chapter 2, "Build a Selection Team That Works," instructs you in building the all-important, cross-functional selection team.

- Chapter 3, "Get the Basic Foundations Right," identifies the key governance and capacity-benchmarking steps required to obtain an optimal selection result.

CHAPTER 1

Craft a No-Bullshit Business Case

Many enterprise project teams sense intuitively that they need a new solution and then figure out how to justify it. This is backward thinking. Instead, you should start with the business case and then proceed directly from there. A solid business case will not only challenge your assumptions around the type and complexity of the tools you need, but also give you a clearer sense of direction and purpose.

Foundation for Any New Technology

Let's be clear: you *do* need a real business case. All major technology efforts beget tough decisions and difficult trade-offs, so it is best to have a business plan in place as a touchstone to keep the team focused—especially if your CFO will be writing big checks to outside vendors.

> **CAUTION** **EXCEL CONTORTIONS**
>
> Many quantitative business cases represent artificial exercises with mythical person-hour cost savings or exaggerated revenue bumps, all via extreme contortions in Excel. That may suffice for obtaining funding approval, but it is not actually a business case and will offer few hints about how to structure and run your technology selection process.
>
> If you can project truly realistic, quantifiable gains, then do so. But in many cases, your business case will rely on nonquantifiable objectives, including improved customer loyalty, better employee morale, or reduced risk of future litigation. To any visionary leadership, these should matter, too. Above all, don't warp the data to show some mythical outcome in a spreadsheet. That's demeaning for you and your colleagues—and leaves you exposed when financial benefits don't fully materialize.

All technology projects can be justified in terms of some combination of the following:

- **Reduced risk:** You will mitigate against compliance and legal troubles or outright disasters. Many records management and security technology solutions apply this rationale.

- **Value creation:** You will generate more revenue or customer loyalty. Ecommerce, salesforce automation, and most digital marketing solutions will use this approach.

- **Greater efficiency:** You will be able to produce more work with the same or fewer people. HR management and ERP (enterprise resource planning) solutions often sell against this justification.

- **Qualitative transformation:** Your enterprise can pursue radically different business models. Social ideation and Q&A technology often rely on this rationale.

Most enterprises seek a combination of these goals, but you should understand that a single technology is unlikely to bring all four. The key is to figure out your top two to three business objectives and keep them front and center throughout a selection process whose tactical complexities tend to distract project leaders from original business goals. Consider this example for a dealer portal at a financial services firm:

1. Lower costs via self-service delivery of digitized marketing collateral.

2. Increase revenue by expanding share of dealer book of business by injecting promotional information into transactional environments.

3. Reduce risk by distributing compliance updates more rapidly and comprehensively.

A time will come when the selection team will disagree on a particular approach. In the previous example, perhaps one of the portal technology offerings excels at dealer-to-dealer collaboration. Being able to go back to your list of top business objectives can help clarify the right decision. In this case, collaboration (however laudable) was not a prime objective, so the team should downplay that capability in their assessment.

Types of Formal Business Cases

Technology projects are seldom cheap. To be sure, the new system can increase value and productivity; however, the initial investment may well require justification in its own right, usually in the form of a written business case.

There are different ways to build a business case for implementing any technology solution. One approach looks at return on investment (ROI) or its cousin, internal rate of return (IRR). This approach entails demonstrating the financial return on your investment, and it is a very powerful justification—if you can credibly predict attractive financial returns.

The After-the-Implementation Business Case

We get calls all of the time from potential clients asking for help in writing a business case for new technology. A recent call from a global media company surprised us because their request for help writing their business case was coming months after they had already purchased and implemented the technology!

It is all too common for leadership to start questioning the rationale of new technology once it reaches the time when the technology was supposed to start delivering value to the organization.

No matter how many meetings or conversations with the appropriate stakeholders getting consensus on the need for new technology, nothing beats having a business case on paper that can be referenced when fingers get pointed if things don't go as expected.

Lesson: No matter how obvious you think your need for technology is, always document your business case for future reference.

Another approach classifies a major expense as a necessary precondition for doing business—such as investing in an upgraded phone system—in circumstances where there is no immediately definable ROI. This is known as a *cost of doing business* (CDB) analysis. A common and quite successful business rationale for some technology is, "We just couldn't go on without one anymore." This is how phones, then faxes, then email, and finally instant messaging got into the enterprise: you simply couldn't work without them.

Both approaches offer valid analytical models for constructing a business case (see Table 1.1). When all else fails, try articulating the implications of doing *absolutely nothing*: what does it mean for employees, customers, and partners going forward?

CAUTION **ROI CALCULATORS**

Many vendors offer preset ROI calculators. These can be helpful to orient your thinking, but a savvy manager will take their assumed labor savings or revenue increases with a grain of salt. ROI calculators also chronically underestimate the additional effort involved in implementing and then managing the new solution itself.

TABLE 1.1   ROI/IRR VS. CDB

	ROI/IRR Return on Investment/ Internal Rate of Return	CDB Cost of Doing Business
Definition	Calculate the value of an investment by dividing incremental revenue + cost savings by the amount invested.	For any company certain investments must be made as a precondition for successfully conducting business.
Classic Example	Rolling out a traditional, direct-marketing campaign. Marginal sales increases can be measured against incremental costs.	Firewalls. You must connect to public networks to do business, but also secure your information systems from outside intrusion.
When to use?	Use when there are clear cause-and-effect outcomes and incremental revenues or cost savings can be readily quantified. For IRR, look at the opportunity costs of not implementing a system.	Use when key arguments cannot be quantified as readily. This technology is a precondition for other corporate revenue and cost-cutting initiatives, rather than vice versa.
Possible Document Management Benefits	Greater sales, broader offerings, reduced customer service costs, reduced content production costs, reduced legal liability, faster time to market, faster e-discovery, and better adaptation.	Better internal collaboration, more fulfilled and specialized staff, greater customer loyalty, broader future business opportunities, less risk of public failure.
Decision-makers likely to concur	Finance-oriented, data driven	Strategic, visionary, intuitive

Understanding True Costs

"How much will this system cost us overall?" Everyone wants to know. The cynic will reply, "Whatever you've budgeted, and then some."

In practice, you can exert great control over costs, which will tend to relate directly to:

- The complexity and richness of the system
- The depth pace of your digital ambitions (doing more/better/ faster costs more)
- The quality of your digital program and product management
- The extent of your migration from an incumbent environment

Your long-term TCO (total cost of ownership) will revolve around three large buckets:

1. Licensing and annual maintenance and support, plus potentially separate hosting fees
2. Implementation, training, and migration
3. Ongoing enhancements, fixes, and upgrades

Don't estimate #3. Often, the year two and three expense of operating and innovating on a platform exceed the initial implementation in year one.

Technology prices—like the vendors themselves—are all over the map. In general, vendors will try to align costs to usage, but sometimes they will try to capture a portion of the business value as well. You can expect costs to vary across:

- Users (named or concurrent)
- Storage or database record volume
- Transaction volumes or API calls
- Data throughput
- CPU utilization or cloud equivalent
- Domains/geographic zones
- Support levels

- Connectors

- Optional modules

- Development, staging, and fail-over environments

In planning your growth scenarios, consider how a particular product's scalability matches up against your overall architecture. This is good practice for performance reasons, but will also affect potential license fee growth as well.

For traditional software, you should budget for support and maintenance costs ranging from 16–24% of the price of all software you purchased, on an annual basis.

> **CAUTION** **SUPPORT VS. UPGRADES**
>
> Make sure that your maintenance and support will cover upgrades, including major upgrades, as some vendors have tried to argue that particular major version upgrades represent "new" products. Don't put up with that.
>
> At the same time, don't expect that covered software upgrades mean no cost to you, since larger installations typically require consulting help from the vendor to migrate to the new version— after all, who else knows how?

One factor in varying maintenance costs is that most vendors offer separate tiers of support at different price levels. Buyers tend to underestimate their support needs; remember that even cloud-based services can go down at any time. One strategy is to seek a higher tier of service, but then try to negotiate the rate down. After a contract is signed, the vendor will want to deliver the software quickly. This is partly so that they can invoice you, but also because many contracts state that the support meter starts ticking the day you take delivery, unless you pre-negotiate a later install date.

You can see two hypothetical examples in Figures 1.1 and 1.2 (both with a low and high of five-year TCOs), on-premise versus a SaaS (software-as-a-service)-based solution. Use them for structure rather than guidance on actual costs because your costs will vary.

WCM Estimate - LOW	ON-PREMISE					
CATEGORY	YEAR ONE	YEAR TWO	YEAR THREE	YEAR FOUR	YEAR FIVE	5-YR TCO
New Software License	$ 120,000	$ -	$ 60,000		$ 60,000	$ 240,000
Total Maint & Support Fees @ 15%	$ 18,000	$ 18,000	$ 27,000	$ 27,000	$ 36,000	$ 126,000
Total Hosting*	$ 48,000	$ 50,400	$ 52,920	$ 55,566	$ 58,344	$ 265,230
Pro Svcs: Fix, Upgrade, Train**	$ -	$ 60,000	$ -	$ 60,000	$ -	$ 120,000
Total Internal Dev Staffing***	$ 80,000	$ 84,000	$ 88,200	$ 92,610	$ 97,241	$ 442,051
Major Implementation & Migration****	$ 240,000	$ 120,000	$ 120,000	$ 120,000	$ 120,000	$ 720,000
Subtotal CAPEX	$ 360,000	$ 120,000	$ 180,000	$ 120,000	$ 180,000	$ 960,000
Subtotal OPEX	$ 146,000	$ 212,400	$ 168,120	$ 235,176	$ 191,585	$ 953,281
OVERALL TOTALS:	$ 506,000	$ 332,400	$ 348,120	$ 355,176	$ 371,585	$ 1,913,281

* Assume host on-premise at $48k/year total cost with 5% increase per year
** Minor improvements outsourced to vendor or SI
*** 0.5 developers at $160/year fully-loaded cost and 5% raises
**** Major implementations/upgrades by SI. Migration with enhancements yearly thereafter

WCM Estimate - HIGH	ON-PREMISE					
CATEGORY	YEAR ONE	YEAR TWO	YEAR THREE	YEAR FOUR	YEAR FIVE	YEAR FIVE
New Software License	$ 240,000	$ -	$ 100,000		$ 100,000	$ 440,000
Total Maint & Support Fees @25%	$ 60,000	$ 60,000	$ 85,000	$ 85,000	$ 110,000	$ 400,000
Total Hosting @ $10k/mo*	$ 150,000	$ 150,000	$ 150,000	$ 150,000	$ 150,000	$ 750,000
Pro Svcs: Fix, Upgrade, Train**	$ -	$ 90,000	$ -	$ 90,000	$ -	$ 180,000
Total Internal Dev Staffing***	$ 240,000	$ 252,000	$ 264,600	$ 277,830	$ 291,722	$ 1,326,152
Major Implementation & Migration****	$ 720,000	$ 240,000	$ 240,000	$ 240,000	$ 240,000	$ 1,680,000
Subtotal CAPEX	$ 960,000	$ 240,000	$ 340,000	$ 240,000	$ 340,000	$ 2,120,000
Subtotal OPEX	$ 450,000	$ 552,000	$ 499,600	$ 602,830	$ 551,722	$ 2,656,152
OVERALL TOTALS:	$ 1,410,000	$ 792,000	$ 839,600	$ 842,830	$ 891,722	$ 4,776,152

* Assume outsource hosting at $105k/month
** Minor improvements outsourced to vendor or SI
*** 1.5 developers at $160/year fully-loaded cost and 5% raises
**** Major implementations/upgrades by SI. Migration with enhancements yearly thereafter

FIGURE 1.1

Total cost of ownership over five years "high" and "low" estimates for an on-premise WCM implementation.

WCM Estimate - LOW	SaaS					
CATEGORY	YEAR ONE	YEAR TWO	YEAR THREE	YEAR FOUR	YEAR FIVE	5-YR TCO
New Software License (incl)	$ -	$ -	$ -		$ -	$ -
Total Maint & Support Fees	$ 96,000	$ 105,600	$ 116,160	$ 127,776	$ 140,554	$ 586,090
Total Hosting*	$ -	$ -	$ -	$ -	$ -	$ -
Pro Svcs: Fix, Upgrade, Train**	$ -	$ 60,000	$ -	$ 60,000	$ -	$ 120,000
Total Internal Dev Staffing***	$ 80,000	$ 84,000	$ 88,200	$ 92,610	$ 97,241	$ 442,051
Major Implementation & Migration****	$ 240,000	$ 120,000	$ 120,000	$ 120,000	$ 120,000	$ 720,000
Subtotal CAPEX	$ 240,000	$ 120,000	$ 120,000	$ 120,000	$ 120,000	$ 720,000
Subtotal OPEX	$ 176,000	$ 249,600	$ 204,360	$ 280,386	$ 237,794	$ 1,148,140
OVERALL TOTALS:	$ 416,000	$ 369,600	$ 324,360	$ 400,386	$ 357,794	$ 1,868,140

* Included
** Minor improvements outsourced to SaaS vebdir
*** 0.5 developers at $160/year fully-loaded cost and 5% raises
**** Major implementations/upgrades by SaaS vendor. Migration with enhancements yearly thereafter

WCM Estimate - HIGH	SaaS					
CATEGORY	YEAR ONE	YEAR TWO	YEAR THREE	YEAR FOUR	YEAR FIVE	YEAR FIVE
New Software License (incl)	$ -	$ -	$ -	$ -	$ -	$ -
Total Maint & Support Fees	$ 240,000	$ 264,000	$ 290,400	$ 319,440	$ 351,384	$ 1,465,224
Total Hosting (incl)	$ -	$ -	$ -	$ -	$ -	$ -
Pro Svcs: Fix, Upgrade, Train**	$ -	$ 90,000	$ -	$ 90,000	$ -	$ 180,000
Total Internal Dev Staffing***	$ 160,000	$ 168,000	$ 176,400	$ 185,220	$ 194,481	$ 884,101
Major Implementation & Migration****	$ 720,000	$ 240,000	$ 240,000	$ 240,000	$ 240,000	$ 1,680,000
Subtotal CAPEX	$ 720,000	$ 240,000	$ 240,000	$ 240,000	$ 240,000	$ 1,680,000
Subtotal OPEX	$ 400,000	$ 522,000	$ 466,800	$ 594,660	$ 545,865	$ 2,529,325
OVERALL TOTALS:	$ 1,120,000	$ 762,000	$ 706,800	$ 834,660	$ 785,865	$ 4,209,325

* Included
** Minor improvements outsourced to vendor or SI
*** 1.0 developers at $160/year fully-loaded cost and 5% raises
**** Major implementations/upgrades by SaaS vendor. Migration with enhancements yearly thereafter

FIGURE 1.2

Five-year TCO for a SaaS implementation. Note that year one costs go down, but over the term, overall cost doesn't differ much from on-premise; the CAPEX:OPEX ratio is more heavily weighted toward the latter, however.

CAUTION SERVICES FEES MAY PREDOMINATE

Be sure to budget for professional services, which in larger enterprise environments can represent 75–90% of your overall expenses. With the exception of the simplest tools, it takes people to get a platform up and running properly for you.

For example, don't be surprised if initial migration costs present the largest portion of your implementation costs. Yet, migration costs also typically prove the most "unknowable" in advance. As part of any selection and PoC (proof of concept) process, be sure to do a trial sample migration and pilot implementation so that both you and the implementer have a greater sense of what the final level of effort will entail.

Tips

- Clearly document the top three or four business objectives for the new technology to guide your selection and implementation teams going forward.

- Consider CDB as an alternative to ROI calculations for business justification.

- Be sure to articulate the costs and impact of doing nothing at all.

- You should remain diligent in your cost negotiations and plan for expansion carefully.

- Recognize that implementation and ongoing enhancements are likely to comprise the lion's share of your long-term TCO and budget accordingly.

CHAPTER 2

Build a Selection Team That Works

Perhaps the most common pitfall of technology selection is the absence of an organized team that represents the varied interests and authority of internal stakeholders. Without a recognized authority, decisions can get made on an ad hoc basis, or you end up defaulting to an incumbent tool, even though it's not a good fit. Worse yet, key conflicts often get postponed throughout the early stages of the project, leading to fierce debates that emerge only after it's time to pick vendor finalists.

So a smart business leader will identify key "stakeholder" groups: those who should participate in or will otherwise be significantly impacted by your selection effort. Some team members will need to be involved in the project directly, while others may just need to be kept informed. For example, you may not need a security expert full-time on the team, but you will want their input or validation at key points.

Note that key influencers among stakeholder groups may not be those who have positions of importance in your organization, but they could still prove essential to your success. We see a growing consensus that the most effective applications result from a truly user-centered design process, with the people who will actually use the system involved from the very beginning to shape the ultimate solution. So be sure to include people who will want to get their hands dirty testing the new system.

> ### CAUTION ONE-DIMENSIONAL TEAM
>
> We sometimes see a temptation among individual IT and business departments to either dominate the selection process themselves or alternatively abdicate completely to the other party. You don't want either path: both groups have a stake in the outcome, and they need to work together for enterprise success.
>
> Also, if all key stakeholders participate in the selection of the solution, they will be much more likely to participate actively in "selling" it to the rest of the enterprise and engage fully for a successful implementation.

Sample Team Composition

So what might a selection team look like? It depends to some extent on the scope and nature of the solution being procured. Let's take two example technology selections:

1. Cloud-based marketing automation

2. On-premise HR management system

For cloud-based marketing automation, the team might consist of:

- VP Marketing (executive sponsor)
- Director Digital Marketing (team chair)
- Manager, Outbound Marketing
- Manager, Customer Relationship Management
- Manager, Content Strategy and Personalization
- Manager, Marketing Analytics
- Marketing Business Analyst
- Lead MarTech Developer
- MarTech Project Manager (PM)
- Enterprise Architect

For the on-premise HR management system, the composition might be different:

- VP HR (executive sponsor)
- Director, HR Operations (team chair)
- Manager, Employee Engagement
- Manager, Employee Benefits
- Manager, Recruitment
- Manager, Employee Professional Development
- Finance Department Liaison
- Enterprise Architect
- Lead HR Systems Developer
- HR Project Manager (PM)

- Manager, Systems Security

- Manager, Enterprise Data Warehousing

- Procurement Department Liaison

Your roles will vary, and in some cases, the enterprise may seek wider participation from legal or financial teams. Smaller enterprises can get away with smaller selection teams. The main point is that people with different expertise and responsibilities should have input into the process, although a business leader ultimately drives the decision-making with significant IT input.

Larger enterprises and most public-sector organizations may possess a specialized procurement department. It's useful to involve this team and leverage their expertise and negotiating skills, but we urge you to retain project direction in the business unit that is leading the selection effort. In our experience, busy procurement groups are all too happy to let you run with the selection project—as long as you can demonstrate a methodical process—which, of course, after reading this book you will.

The other thing you'll notice is that the teams are not "top-heavy" and instead emphasize working-level knowledge. This approach leads to more practical outcomes—and is also more realistic since the selection methodology we propose will prove to be very hands-on—but it also presumes that team decision-making will align properly with larger enterprise objectives. That, in turn, depends on governance, which we'll tackle in Chapter 3, " Get the Basic Foundations Right."

Stakeholder Extremes

You'll want to involve a wide array of people early in the selection process. In fact, getting people's thoughts on what is working well and not working well early in the process is the first step in the change management associated with rolling out new technology.

However, the key is to find the right balance between too many and not enough (of the right) stakeholders.

Consider these two extremes we've witnessed:

- One client decided that their CMO and CTO would become the sole representatives in the selection process because they "knew exactly what the organization needed."

  This proved to be problematic for several reasons. First, the staff members who would actually use the new technology on a daily basis would feel disinvested and resentful of being told what they needed to use to do their job. Second, with minimal stakeholders, the process would inevitably become limited in scope and prone to the schedule challenges of two busy people.

- There was another instance where we encountered an auditorium full of stakeholders: literally more than 60 people on the selection team! The problem with this method was that we were forced to use a numerical scoring survey to take the pulse of the stakeholders, and this came at the expense of having a reasonable discourse about what everyone liked and didn't like.

Lesson: Find the right blend of leadership and actual practitioners—ideally, 8–12 people.

Tips

- If you haven't already done so, recruit an executive-level business champion to sponsor the initiative going forward.

- Involve key business stakeholders earlier rather than later, with multiple departments actively involved.

- Create a representative selection team that reports to a program champion via a program chair with a separate project manager to deal with logistics and planning.

- Procurement departments can bring useful PM, bidder communications, and negotiating experience to the table, which you should leverage, while retaining business leadership of the overall selection process.

- Make sure that the interests of your customers, employees, partners, or other stakeholders are adequately represented.

- Don't make the team too "top-heavy" with senior leadership who may not have the time or specialized expertise to participate effectively.

CHAPTER 3

Get the Basic Foundations Right

S election teams should never work in a vacuum: the key is to establish a clear approach to decision-making to keep the process moving and ensure that decisions reflect broader enterprise priorities.

At the same time, you need to make sure that you have an accurate picture of enterprise maturity and capabilities to incorporate new digital tooling. What is your realistic capacity to exploit new technology?

Establish Governance and Decision-Making

"Governance" can be an intimidating concept—but it need not be daunting to you. At its core, governance really just means *having consistent structures for making decisions*. If you can't make decisions in a legitimate, methodical way, your project will get nowhere.

Ideally, the governance of your technology selection and implementation effort will dovetail with existing technology or business governance frameworks in your organization. If those don't exist, you may need to create them. Most governance frameworks establish senior-level policy-making bodies with more working-level operational bodies reporting to them (see Figure 3.1).

In the context of technology procurement, the steering committee sets the overall budget and business objectives, while the selection team runs the actual procurement. Many enterprises already use technology review boards to validate technology decisions, and these can serve as effective steering committees, as long as the project business champion is a member.

If you have a smart selection team chair and project manager, they will keep the steering committee regularly apprised of progress and milestones, and will carefully achieve validation on key decisions in the process. However, make sure that you don't overinvolve executive leadership in the process: for one thing, they don't have enough time or relevant knowledge to make tactical decisions. Again, this can be very culturally specific, so look to other projects in your enterprise that managed this balancing act successfully.

Enterprise Business
Strategies

Compliance
Requirements

Steering **Committee(s):**
Direction, Alignment, and Resources

Cross-Unit Working Teams:
Tactics and Programs

Program and Product
Management

Education, Support,
Advice

FIGURE 3.1

Here is a typical, two-tiered enterprise technology governance structure with a steering committee overseeing a more tactical working group. In our case, it may be a technology review board overseeing a technology selection committee.

So how should your selection team make vendor-filtering decisions? You actually have many different choices, as shown in Table 3.1.

In our work facilitating selection team decision-making, we've tended to favor consensus as the most productive approach, with the caveat that it can be useful to take "micro-votes" on certain contributing factors (e.g., "Which vendor did best on Test Case #2?"). When you cannot achieve consensus, you often encourage a kind of fiat, where the project champion or steering committee gets presented with a fair summary of the disagreements on the selection team and ultimately makes the decision.

TABLE 3.1 CONTRASTING DECISION-MAKING OPTIONS

	PROS	CONS
CONSENSUS Decide based on what's at least minimally acceptable to nearly all members.	Bodes well for future harmony and most readily justifiable to superiors.	Might not prove to be the best decision, especially if it's watered down via compromise.
VOTING Decide based on what the majority wants.	Efficient and seems fair.	Ignores potentially decisive expertise or concerns of the losing minority members; for example, should all votes be equal?
FIAT Decide based on a leader's wishes.	Simple and aligns decisions with actual power structures.	Feels arbitrary and risky, and bodes poorly for future staff support.
FORMULA Decide based on team scoring.	Transparent and seems scientific.	Excessively rigid and inadequately accounts for intangible factors or blocking concerns.
UNANIMITY Decide when everyone agrees.	Creates unambiguous conclusion.	Rarely achievable and risks deadlock.

We often see enterprises (especially public-sector organizations) use complex, weighted spreadsheets, where team members enter in ratings or other data, with built-in formulas spitting out a winner. This is a mistake.

Some quantitative data should certainly feed into your decision, e.g., pricing or transaction speeds. However, depending on crude formulas in a world where intangible factors and gating considerations can prove decisive only gives you the illusion of scientific validity.

A formulaic approach brings several difficult problems:

- Small inaccuracies in formulas can lead to big variations in outcomes.

- Truly accurate weighting is impossible (e.g., Should architectural fit really be 10% or 20% of the total?).

- How do you over-/underweight different people's opinions in a world where team members have different sets of expertise?

- How do you weight essential "gating" (no-go or must-have) considerations (e.g., around security)?

- Spreadsheets don't readily accommodate key qualitative intangibles, like usability and organizational fit.

In the end, here's what typically happens: selection team members modify their scores to get the desired outcomes. A better approach features a meaningful discussion of trade-offs, using understanding and negotiation to get to the best decision. In Chapter 12, "How to Evaluate Proposals Critically," we'll show you a structured approach to decision-making that employs vendor rankings rather than ratings.

While all this discussion of decision-making amid potential disagreements may seem a bit discouraging right now, be reassured that pursuing an iterative, user-centered, test-based approach as prescribed in the rest of this book will go a long way toward bringing greater clarity to your team's decisions. Following this approach, many a customer has said, "In the end, it was obvious which vendor to pick!"

Measure Capacity: Be Honest!

You may have great digital ambitions, but how likely will you or your enterprise be able to fulfill them? Do you have the requisite skills in house, do you have the requisite culture to manage change effectively, and do you have the resources, time, expertise, and commitment to see the initiative through? Try to take a candid look at your own readiness, as well as assess and pre-empt potential project risks that could derail your efforts.

Your capability to obtain business value from new technology will depend on closing two gaps (see Figure 3.2):

1. **Hyperbole:** The gap between what vendors say their tools can do and what they actually excel at in real life

2. **Capacity:** The gap between what the tools can really do and your ability to truly leverage those services

In this book, you'll find a methodology for closing the hyperbole gap through a user-centered, no-bullshit process for testing the tools upfront. But before you even go there, you need to clearly understand your enterprise capacity—both current limitations and future opportunities.

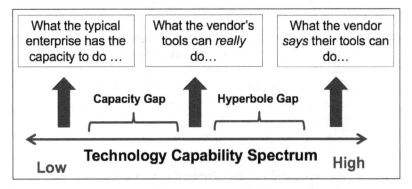

FIGURE 3.2

Any enterprise selecting new technology has to mind two gaps: hyperbole and capacity. Failure to close the capacity gap can lead to project and budget crises.

To realistically understand your existing capacity, you should audit, assess and explain your current state through a benchmarking exercise. Ideally, you should benchmark your current situation against a structured model and against other enterprises. At a minimum, you must benchmark your people, information, systems, and processes.

Benchmarking your digital environments against a model—like a maturity or effectiveness model—can give you a structured baseline to measure your effectiveness in a variety of areas (see Figure 3.3).

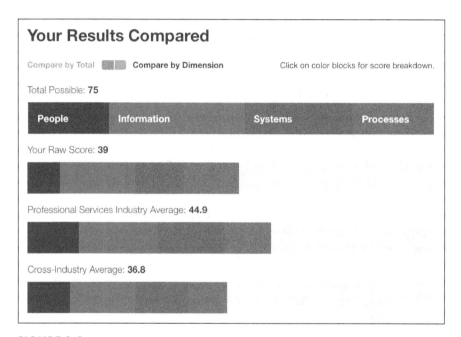

FIGURE 3.3
Analyze your own capabilities and benchmark yourself versus a structured model and versus your industry and cross-industry peers.

Benchmarking your digital environments against other enterprises shows where you are outperforming or lagging behind your peers and can shine light on where you are over- and underinvesting in one dimension or another, so you can rebalance your portfolio of capabilities.

For more information and examples, see **www.realstorygroup.com /RealScore**.

REAL STORY

At Real Story Group, we worked with a global manufacturing firm that was struggling with its existing distributor and customer portal environment. The technology was aging, the smallish vendor couldn't keep up, and growing demands from the field were increasingly unmet.

The firm asked us to investigate swapping out their incumbent platform with a new portal technology framework. But a deeper examination uncovered that, while their existing platform was surely a misfit, the company faced more serious constraints that were not technical in nature:

- The absence of a unified taxonomy prohibited meaningful systems integration.

- A lack of digital savvy among the customer relationship teams prevented them from exploiting the tools they already had.

- No governance structures existed to prioritize feature requests, leading to squeaky-wheel roadmaps and system bloat.

We counseled them to wait at least a year before obtaining new technology and to use that time to address the all-important "soft" issues around digital capacity and readiness for innovation in the organization.

Lesson: New technology will not put your organizational house in order. First, make sure that you address your capacity gaps and then acquire new tools.

Tips

- Try wherever possible to leverage and extend existing decision-making bodies.

- Don't ignore or postpone addressing governance shortcomings.

- Don't create an overelaborate governance structure.

- Never exclude diverse IT interests (systems, security, development, architecture) from decision-making.

- Never abdicate decision-making just to IT, and place a businessperson to chair decision-making bodies.

- Take a candid measure of your internal abilities and resources, and gauge your organization's appetite for risk.

- Make sure that you measure your true capacity to implement new digital technology successfully before embarking on any selection.

PART II

Needs and Opportunities

After establishing a solid business case, enterprises will typically turn to assembling the oft-dreaded "requirements document"—or more accurately, a set of documents, spreadsheets, and diagrams that compose a multiheaded requirements package.

Large requirements packages actually provide a false sense of security. Modern digital technology entails real people interacting with screens. Technology selection leaders need to capture those interactive requirements, but also remain realistic at this phase about their inability to fully know what their enterprise really needs and will adopt eventually.

This section will show how long spreadsheets full of "what" requirements really don't work, and instead will focus on "how" a solution might work. The best way to reveal key differences among suppliers is to craft narrative "user stories" with "personas" (rough equivalent to use-cases with actors).

In other words, *tell testable stories*. Business users have stories; so do customers, partners, developers, sysadmins, designers, auditors, and others.

This section will lead you through an approach to telling those stories in a way that's more conducive to differentiating among technology suppliers.

- Chapter 4, "Capture Requirements That Don't Suck," shows you how *not* to document requirements and introduces key concepts in information gathering and user-centered design.

- Chapter 5, "Why User Stories Are Everything," explains how to craft testable stories that will serve as your core vehicle for differentiating among solutions.

- Chapter 6, "Ask Questions That Really Matter," offers a simple approach to converting static requirements into interactive questions in order to glean relevant information from prospective bidders.

CHAPTER 4

Capture Requirements That Don't Suck

A solid understanding of your organization's requirements is essential to project success. Getting that understanding will involve information gathering from various stakeholder groups, potentially utilizing a variety of techniques.

Note that at this stage, your requirements should be business- and user-focused, rather than detailed technical specifications. (We'll get to those in Chapter 6, "Ask Questions That Really Matter.") The final key step here is to analyze and prioritize your requirements, in order to determine which ones to emphasize in the RFP (request for proposal) and subsequent demos and bake-offs.

How *Not* to Articulate Requirements

Whatever you do, avoid "check box" requirements sheets where you ask the vendor: "Can you do this, can you do that?"

As a practical matter, vendors have seen all these questions and have figured out how to check all the boxes. But what's worse is that such spreadsheets convert the understanding of what should be a human-centered, interactive activity into a bloodless series of row-by-row activities better suited for robots repeatedly performing rote tasks.

The typical pitfall here starts like this: a business analyst (BA) goes around interviewing users and other stakeholders, and she ends up with a long wish list of features. Excel allows her to categorize those features, which is handy, but because of the limitless rows, her spreadsheet will tend to emphasize comprehensiveness over business impact.

To address the challenge of priorities, the typical enterprise process asks stakeholders to rank their needs, perhaps on a scale of 1 to 5, or using MoSCoW (Must Have/Should Have/Could Have/Won't Have) or some other methodology. Not surprisingly, this generates a scrum where users compete to identify as many rows of "Must Haves" as possible.

Ultimately, someone will ask the BA to tie back each requirement row to the business case (remember that?), so she then spends several days building new tables and cross-references in Excel. Ultimately, reviewers find exceptions and variants for each feature, so new columns get added. Now the spreadsheet is too big to fit on a standard screen, let alone print out. It's impressive...and impressively unhelpful.

CAUTION DON'T INCLUDE THE KITCHEN SINK

While it's critical to identify your requirements, it will prove even more important to *prioritize* them. Noncritical requirements can hijack the product selection process by distracting you and your vendors from what's really important.

Remember that you are *not specifying out an actual implementation* at this phase. You are trying to contrast potential suppliers and solutions. So while complete requirements are nice, *prioritized* requirements are gold.

We've seen many a project stall very early in the process when enterprises get bogged down in the minutia of trying to unearth every possible requirement.

The most successful enterprises hone in on what we call *differentiating requirements*. Differentiating requirements describe use cases that are truly unique for your enterprise. Differentiating requirements are also the types of requirements that elicit very different solutions from the various vendors in the marketplace.

Knowing which user journeys and outcomes are more important than others will make it easier to distinguish among vendors. It will also help you keep costs in line with your budget. Remember that excessive wish lists lead to scope-creep, overbuying, implementation delays, and ultimately, budget-busting.

Applying UCD Principles

There's a different way to do this than torturing your BA— and everyone else—with long spreadsheets, and it revolves around pursuing a user-centered design (UCD) approach that emphasizes narratives, which we'll call *stories* here. People will disagree about the tactics of UCD, but we can generalize overall that a user-centered approach is:

- **Holistic** to encompass the entire digital experience (and therefore not feature based)

- **Iterative**, where you initially sketch light (and therefore imperfect) requirements and refine them over time via iteration

- **Story-based**, with an emphasis on user narratives, often called "journeys" or "top tasks"

The Government Agency with the Massive Checklist

We once advised a major U.S. federal government agency to select a new portal platform as a hub for small business advice. We came late to the process after an initial round of vendor demos had failed to differentiate clearly among the bidders.

The problem was Excel. Or more specifically, the entire RFP as a 10-tab worksheet, with some sheets going hundreds of rows deeps. Most of the tabs held feature requests—notably categorized by agency department rather than customer persona—with a long series of columns annotating those features. (Our favorite: the ever-beloved "Must be easy to use" requirement.) Nearly all the features were listed as "must have." They were rigorously cross-tabbed to a long but vague set of business objectives, but otherwise there was no prioritization.

The vendors didn't know what to demo, although several gamely tried. Mostly, they just talked about their (voluminous) proposal responses, most of which consisted of declaring, for each row, "We can do that!"

Ultimately, we were able to recraft a more user-centered approach, with a narrower scope, that vendors could reasonably demo against.

Lesson: Stay away from long, feature-based checklists.

There's much more to UCD, but for our purposes, two key constructs stand out:

- **Personas:** User archetypes that guide decisions about technology effectiveness. Personas are useful in the sense that they create a common shared understanding of the user group, but with a human existence to help keep it real.

- **User Stories:** A to-be story about the "daily life of" or a journey undertaken by key personas. User stories are exceptionally valuable here because they offer test cases against which you can compare and contrast vendor bidders.

Information Gathering

You can chose from among numerous well-known methods for eliciting information needed to create personas and user stories.

- **Document reviews:** Including existing and prospective systems diagrams, planning documents, and analytics, but also the information that flows through the anticipated technology, like catalog entries for an ecommerce site, or forms in a document management system

- **Questionnaires:** Including customer and employee surveys, as well as specialized questions you might want to pose in advance of any in-person meetings

- **Workshops:** A useful way to debrief groups of people, as well as experiment with more forward-looking brainstorming; customer focus groups fall into this category as well

- **Interviewing:** Debriefing individual stakeholders one-on-one, where they may become more candid

- **Shadowing:** Following stakeholders around for a typical duration of time; this sort of contextual inquiry is often the most useful, but also labor intensive

- Potentially others...

Different practitioners will take different approaches, and clearly the level of effort here should be commensurate with the anticipated benefits and risks with the new technology.

At Real Story Group when we're creating personas and scenarios, we like to take a modified contextual inquiry approach. We gather individuals with similar roles in a conference room and debrief the team as a group. Using a projector, we may ask some members to log in to show specific examples of an incumbent system to the group. When we are gathering requirements for an interactive system, we make the environment as interactive as possible to get the maximum information exchange.

We'll send five questions in advance as the agenda for the workshop:

1. Show us briefly, on the screen, what you do.

2. What works well in the existing environment (top three only)?

3. What doesn't work well or is missing in the existing environment (top three only)?

4. How is your work/market/environment/customer changing?

5. What else is important that we haven't discussed?

The questions are deliberately open ended, to create as much of an open dialogue as possible. Note the emphasis on "top three"—we don't want a laundry list of features, but rather the most important problems and opportunities.

Sometimes, it's hard for line employees to identify potential future opportunities, so it can be useful to introduce the whole process with an educational workshop describing industry best practices or examples of what other enterprises have done with the technology. This is particularly important when selecting a type of technology that the enterprise has never used before.

The question still remains of staying aligned with the initial business plan. We like to book half-hour sessions with interested executives to understand the broader business currents and objectives underneath the technology selection effort.

At this point, a lot of raw material has been accumulated. The next step is to convert it into the two core components of the future RFP: user stories and advanced Q&A.

Tips

- You will need to invest in both information and process analysis, and this will require document analysis as well as contextual inquiry.

- Avoid long, undifferentiated, spreadsheet-based feature lists in favor of uncovering material necessary to create key personas and scenarios.

- Start with the user experience and work your way back into enterprise systems.

- Avoid the temptation to broaden your scope beyond the original charter.

- You don't need to be perfect at this (or any other) phase, so focus inquiry into your stakeholders' most burning problems or intense needs.

CHAPTER 5

Why User Stories Are Everything

A t this phase, you can convert requirements into user stories that are intelligible to anyone and are testable throughout the forthcoming selection process. User stories are short, real-life narratives that describe your information, your processes, your people, your customers, and your anticipated business results.

After defining the business case, it's the most important foundational work you will do, so spend some time to get it right—but don't agonize over the details, since you'll have the opportunity to modify them as you learn more throughout the selection process.

How to Structure a User Story

There are many ways to structure user stories and indeed, some software development methodologies offer very specific guidelines. For the purposes of technology selection, we suggest a seven-part structure for each:

1. **Title:** The name of the journey

2. **Task profile/persona:** The person's role, including a named persona to make it more human, typically with limited access rights

3. **Description:** A shorthand sentence to expand on the title

4. **Background:** The setup for the scenario, with useful context

5. **Objective:** What you need to accomplish and why

6. **Narrative:** What happens—a story about what the personas experience and do, including decisions that they make and the outcomes

7. (Optional) **Variant:** Some additional steps that might get addressed during the demo phase only as time allows

Before we get into the meat of the narrative, understand that the RFP background and objective sections of the stories are important setups. The background introduces the personas, provides a "back story" where needed, and helps the readers understand why they are pursuing particular journeys. The objective explicitly tells the readers why the scenario is included at all: the all-important business goal, which should shape how bidders respond.

You want to enter any procurement with a clear list of actors and their roles in any system. For the purposes of this book, we cite the catch-all term "users," but ironically, the one word you want to avoid in your RFP stories is *user*.

Instead, raise up the people who really matter by their specific role: customers, colleagues, customer service reps, managers, prospects, partners, distributors, suppliers, developers, designers, authors, editors, data analysts, community managers, marketers, directors, executives, knowledge managers, line workers—the available list is endless.

For the system you're trying to procure, there's a handful of personas that matter a lot. Call them by name.

The narrative is where all the action happens—where you tell the stories about how the personas interact with each other and the system to achieve certain ends. There is both an art and a science to drafting such narratives. You want to be reasonably detailed, but not prescriptive; for example, you don't specify where a "submit button" appears on a screen, just that "Edna the Editor saves her work prior to publishing."

To the extent possible, narratives should reflect "to-be" journeys and as such are designed to be aspirational. If you know that a particular narrative might present a "stretch" for existing state-of-the-art, that's OK—just signal to the bidders that you know what you've sketched out might be difficult to execute and then see what they come back with.

If you want an "alternate ending" or perhaps a journey needs to go in a different direction, you can include a variant paragraph or two. Resist the urge to go overboard here just to satisfy a squeaky wheel or random edge cases. The more tangents you include, the more you dilute the truly important requirements. We often recommend that bidders don't need to give written answers to variants, but may have to demo them as time allows during the demo or PoC phases.

Example User Story

Here's an example user story. It's a simple one, and yours may prove to be more complicated, but you'll get the gist of it (see Figure 5.1).

4.2.3 Scenario 3: Managing and using media assets

User Task Profile Targeted	Photographer, Site Manager
Subject Personas	Chelsey, Ben
Scenario Description	Managing and manipulating a collection of images

Background:

The University employs a small team of photographers and videographers, and makes increasing use of media assets across its sites.

Chelsey is a University photographer assigned to cover the Business School 2018 Commencement activities. She takes a variety of photos, which she stores offline. She identifies 12 images to "webify" for a collection to be shared on the University website. She crops, scales, filters, and downsamples the images offline.

Objective:

The University wants effective management and manipulation services for web-ready assets, from within our Web CMS platform.

Narrative:

Chelsey uploads the 12 images as a collection into the CMS. She labels the collection, then tags and names each individual image, assigning alt tags, ad-hoc keywords, and certain controlled vocabulary terms. For example, she can select and tag multiple faculty names to each image. The system automatically generates thumbnails and exposes an asset library with suitable sub-folders or subcategories, and repository search, including advanced field search.

Within the CMS, Chelsey navigates to the Business School site and inserts a "Photo Collections" element, which she configures to show the 2018 Commencement photo collection. The photos are displayed as a carousel, or slide show, or similar format. Chelsey adds some relevant narrative text. She previews on staging, then pushes the new content into production.

Ben the website manager receives an automated alert about a new photo collection that's gone live. He wants to link to the photo collection from the home page. However, that home page element template dictates an image of a different size than Chelsey has uploaded. Ben selects one of the images, and–using a browser-based tool in the CMS–crops and scales it further, then saves it as a separate image to represent the collection. He adds that image to the home page element and links from there to the full collection on the Business School subsite.

Optional Variant A:
It is June, and Chelsey runs an annual audit of assets in the CMS repository. She runs a report that indicates images that are in the repository but not linked to or embedded within any page (i.e., do not appear anywhere on the site). These are presented in a list for simple disposition.

FIGURE 5.1

An example user story for a web content management system (CMS) at a public university.

With this user story, the customer has signaled a variety of important requirements, but most importantly, they will be able realize those needs and opportunities in the context of an actual business process that needs to get executed on a regular basis.

There is a bit of art and science when it comes to developing user stories. The trick is to be descriptive of what you want your future state to look like, but you need to do so without being overly prescriptive. You want to leave it open-ended enough so that the vendor can do the prescribing of how their solution best meets your needs. So in your stories, talk about what employees and customers do, but don't go into too much detail about *how* they do it.

Which User Stories and How Many?

How many user stories should you develop? To paraphrase Winston Churchill: all that are necessary, and not one more. Of course, this depends to a large degree on the complexity and importance of the technology you're selecting. If you are procuring a new email platform for a 40,000-person enterprise, you'll want to make sure you've accounted for numerous use cases. If you're selecting accounting software for a mid-sized business, you may have only three or four journeys to address.

If you get tempted to add more than six-to-eight user stories to your selection process, understand that each one you add makes more work for both you and the bidding vendors. It becomes more for them to describe and demo, and more for you to evaluate throughout the process. Note that most user stories involve multiple personas, so you don't need an individual journey for each key persona.

If you find the team wanting to include more than eight, have you really prioritized your requirements against your business goals? Reference your business case and focus on your most important objectives.

Which user stories should you pursue? Here again, you should be guided by your business case—applying new technology to which personas and journeys most effectively satisfy your business objectives.

This will prove highly situational. For example, in an ecommerce platform selection, you will isolate different types of customer journeys (new customer, returning customer, failed transaction, etc.), as well as interweave how your key enterprise colleagues (marketers, merchandizers, customer support staff, designers, etc.) will interact with the platform.

When selecting workplace or customer-facing technology, be sure to include essential IT personas and tasks, such as developers enhancing and testing the platform. Even simpler, SaaS-based products can entail consequences for your internal IT team, including requirements like integration with your single sign-on (SSO) layer. While some of these are one-time challenges best addressed as specific questions (see Chapter 6, "Ask Questions That Really Matter"), to the extent your IT colleagues need to interact with the system regularly, they become important personas and often require their own stories.

Similarly, don't restrict the narrative to just the tool you're procuring. With expanding technology portfolios and the rise of API-driven development, your new platform is unlikely to prove completely free-standing, and instead will need to co-exist within a larger ecosystem of tools. From a user's standpoint, it really shouldn't matter: they have a particular goal and shouldn't have to think about your system boundaries. So follow the story where it goes and instruct each vendor to propose how their piece fits together into your larger whole.

CAUTION DON'T RULE OUT OTHER TYPES OF STORIES

By the time you read this, methodologies around "design thinking" will have evolved. It's early days for this new world of technology requirements definition, and we're seeing a lot of useful experimentation.

In particular, you'll likely find alternatives to user stories. One promising approach is "job stories," which focus on situations, motivations, and outcomes rather than personas, context, and journeys. Doubtless other types of storytelling will emerge as well. We're agnostic on what works best, and you should be, too, as long as your selection process includes a narrative approach to describing interactivity rather than a checklist of features.

As always, know that the iterative process described in the chapters that follow means that you can modify and switch out individual stories as you start to see systems in action. Follow your best initial judgment, *but then give yourself the leeway to adapt.*

For links to example RFPs with completed scenarios, see the appendix, "Resources and Examples."

Tips

- Pay more attention to developing scenarios than "checklist" requirements.

- Use your user stories as the core of your pending RFP (more about RFPs later).

- User stories ideally reflect a "to-be" process, although you may want to document "as-is" as well.

- Do not make user stories overly prescriptive; give the vendor a chance to address your challenges creatively.

- Develop user stories that speak to the needs of each major actor in your pending system, but as always, prioritize the most important journeys.

- Consider user story "variants" or "alternate endings" to address diverse processes, but don't do this just to satisfy myriad "edge cases" that distract from your most decisive requirements.

- In a world of evolving UCD methodologies, you might choose another approach like "job stories"—the important thing is to describe an interactive narrative.

- Perfect is the enemy of good; you'll have a chance to iterate on these user stories throughout the process.

CHAPTER 6

Ask Questions That Really Matter

Thus far, we've been focusing on narrative user stories as the prime mechanism for conveying requirements. Unfortunately, user stories are not always ideal for communicating all needs, particularly those related to technical topics like architecture and integration, or that relate to more operational concerns, like implementation and migration.

Here again, you may become tempted to turn to the dreaded spreadsheet to list those requirements, but we have a better idea. Instead, enumerate these issues not as checklists, but as a series of questions to bidders that will yield a more useful and informative information exchange.

At Real Story Group, we call this "Advanced Questions & Answers," and it fulfills a very important function in sharing critical requirements in a way that encourages differentiation among bidders. In particular you advance the conversation by converting all your "Does your..." checklist items into *How* does your..." questions.

Example Questions

Your questions should have three components:

- Topic
- Background—why are you asking—*very* useful for bidders?
- Questions—what do you want to know?

Here are two example Q&A couplets, from the sample RFP you can find in the appendix, "Resources and Examples."

Example 1: YouTube Integration

Background	XYZ University is populating a YouTube channel with a growing number of videos. We are rolling out a video server solely for internal pedagogic use, but will rely on YouTube for all our public videos for at least the near future.
Questions	Please describe how your system supports integration with YouTube. For example, how can you facilitate the embedding of YouTube videos? Does your system provide capabilities to help manage your YouTube channel?

In this case, we could have woven YouTube into one of the scenarios, but it didn't quite fit, and in any case, we had some more questions around it that needed to get addressed.

Example 2: Active Directory and System Entitlements

Background	XYZ University presently runs one active directory forest on a single domain. We maintain security groups in AD. The university also supports Shibboleth for identity propagation.
Questions	Please describe how you employ AD for authentication and authorization. Can you support a mixed entitlement model where some rights derive from AD and others are set within your system? How can user entitlements management get delegated to individual departments?

Here we *could* have asked in a spreadsheet, "Do you support active directory?" The vendor would have emphatically checked yes, but when you look deeper, you can see that, in fact, we had more complicated concerns, and as usual, the most important dialogue would take place more around *how* than *what*. In any case, the background we provided gave bidders useful information about our environment and concerns so that they could derive the best solution for us more effectively.

Types of Questions to Ask

Typically, the types of questions you need to address in advanced Q&A fall into five categories (see Figure 6.1):

- **Integration services:** Where you will need to connect to other enterprise or partner systems

- **Functional services:** Capabilities that don't fit neatly into one of your user stories

- **System services:** To deal with critical storage, security, network, and related capabilities—less germane for cloud-based solutions, but still always an issue

- **Implementation services:** Not technology related, but likely critical to your success

- **Hosting services:** Where you can optionally break out specific questions about the vendor's preferred cloud environment.

To be sure, you could include any of those aspects in user stories; you could even include an implementation or migration scenario in your requirements. When assisting clients at Real Story Group, we typically include at least one developer user story. By their nature, though, these systems and integration topics sometimes fit more readily into a straightforward, Q&A format.

5.	**Advanced Q&A**	**19**
5.1	**Integration Services**	**19**
5.1.1	Traffic Analytics	19
5.1.2	Site and Application Caching	20
5.1.3	Email and Campaign Management	20
5.1.4	Blogging and WordPress	20
5.1.5	Jira and Project/Change Management	20
5.1.6	CRM-based Knowledgebase	21
5.1.7	Commenting and Other UGC	21
5.1.8	Single Sign-on and System Entitlements	21
5.2	**Functional Services**	**21**
5.2.1	Taxonomy Management Services	21
5.2.2	Sitemap	22
5.2.3	Archiving	22
5.2.4	Advanced Roll-back	22
5.2.5	Repository Search	22
5.2.6	Internal Reporting	22
5.2.7	Mobile Services	23
5.2.8	Forms Services	23
5.2.9	Site Search Services	23
5.2.10	Module/Plugin Services	23
5.3	**System Services**	**24**
5.3.1	External Site Security	24
5.3.2	Support Matrix	24
5.3.3	Overall Architecture	24
5.3.4	Administration and Customization	24
5.3.5	Disaster Recovery	25
5.4	**Professional Systems Integration (Implementation) Services**	**25**
5.4.1	Methodology	25
5.4.2	Rapid Migration	25
5.4.3	Toolset Knowledge	26
5.4.4	Agency Partnerships	26
5.5	**Hosting Options**	**26**

FIGURE 6.1
Sample list of question topic areas from a banking application RFP. This is illustrative of the types of issues where you want to query vendors; you will likely not need this many, but it's a useful tour of the breadth of potential concerns.

Your questions will vary based on the nature and complexity of the technology you want to purchase. Avoid the temptation to ask *too* many questions here, though, lest you fall victim to the same dysfunction of the endless checklist, which dilutes your priorities and could discourage the best vendors from bidding.

In any case, the key questions here revolve around *how*, not *what*. Many competing technology vendors can do the same things—on paper. Where they will tend to differ is in approach and the actual execution of particular features. "How" gets you to essential answers about intent, context, and usability much faster.

"Scalability" is a tricky concept in technology. People will say *scale* when talking about different things, so the term can become vague and take on a marketing-speak quality. Yet for larger enterprises— say, with tens of thousands of employees serving customers across dozens of different marketplaces—the technology choices you face start to become qualitatively different.

So let's review some common challenges of scale you will need to address.

- **Identity management:** Including potentially connecting to multiple different identity stores

- **Global footprint:** Including support for multiple languages and staff matrixed geographically as well as functionally

- **Multiple regulatory and legal constraints:** Larger enterprises need to "play it by the book" in ways that smaller companies often do not

- **Intense information-sharing needs:** Ignoring knowledge sharing is a small-company luxury

- **High usage volumes and variable spikes:** Both for customer- and employee-facing systems (we've seen more systems fall over at enterprise usage rates than we care to remember)

- **Use-case diversity:** Many software platforms can support a single use-case, but very few can deploy a platform that solves business problems across a broad spectrum of user stories, around the world

Addressing Architectural Considerations

Enterprises rarely undertake true "greenfield" technology selections, completely unencumbered by pre-existing platforms and commitments. Any new or replacement technology you adopt needs to fit into a broader architecture. Even if you are selecting a software-as-a-service (SaaS) or other cloud-based vendor, you will likely still have to integrate with other systems, at a minimum, your identity management services.

So what's the best way to describe these requirements? For starters, many such requirements can be readily explained and turned into questions using the advanced Q&A technique described earlier.

More generally, we advise assembling architectural background and diagrams as comprehensively as possible. If they don't yet exist, create both as-is and to-be schematics. Include both logical (what the systems do) and physical (what the systems look like) diagrams.

Enterprise architects can create highly useful artifacts, showing how data and services flow across environments. These help bidders understand and explain more effectively where their tools can fit into your world.

Just make sure that you include narrative explanations that can explain the context for all the boxes and arrows—or be prepared to field a phone call where you fill in bidders during the selection process.

> **CAUTION** **MINIMIZE TECHNOLOGY NON-NEGOTIABLES**
>
> Technical requirements typically beget "must-have" requirements. Sometimes, enterprises will insist on a particular flavor of technology or license model in an effort by the IT team to prefilter out poor architectural fits. We understand this need, particularly when it comes to security consideration, but we also frequently see buyers go overboard here.
>
> This results in unreasonably limited choices for business stakeholders, or a bias toward only the largest and most expensive solutions. In extreme cases, business owners will go out and self-procure a "shadow" solution to avoid these restrictions.
>
> Consider the following examples: do you really need to be rigid?
>
> - **Technology language:** Sure you may have expertise and prefer, say, .NET over Java, but should that really be decisive, especially in an era of API-driven development?
>
> - **License model:** Avoid getting too religious in favor or against open source versus commercial models, especially as they are increasingly converging.
>
> - **Deployment model:** Cloud has rightfully become the default here; make sure you that have an air-tight reason for doing anything on-premise.

When the Shadow System Goes Dark

We worked with a consumer product goods enterprise whose IT department was slow to embrace applications hosted in the Cloud. When some employees wanted to collaborate, they went around their IT department and signed up for a SaaS-based social-collaboration service, which became wildly popular among the employees and spread quickly throughout the enterprise.

Ultimately, the IT department conducted a vetting exercise. When a security flaw was discovered, the enterprise had no choice but to shut the service down completely. Thousands of employees were left upset and frustrated.

Lesson: Even if you have recourse to tools that solve near-term business needs, make sure that you involve your IT and security stakeholders in their selection. IT rules and procedures may be inconvenient, but are often in place for very good reasons.

Tips

- Ask questions rather than delimit "checklist" requirements.

- Ask "how" questions instead of "what," to better illuminate the inner workings of the toolset.

- Use these questions to get to deeper answers around topics that may not be uncovered fully in a demo, such as systems administration and integration, as well as implementation and support methodologies.

- For larger enterprises, make sure that you address the unique challenges of scalability early and often.

- Perfect is the enemy of good; you'll have a chance to iterate on these questions throughout the process.

PART III

Conduct Market Analysis

Which vendors will you engage in your search to conduct market analysis? You definitely want to cast a wider eye than just the suppliers who happen to be contacting you. Indeed, the best fit may come from a vendor you don't even know yet, perhaps within a marketplace you hadn't even considered.

Chapter 7, "Find More Than the Usual Suspects," gives you advice about how to make sure you're looking at the right marketplace to address your business needs, and it contrasts different sources of information and advice.

Once you've zeroed in on a marketplace, Chapter 8, "How to Target the Right Suppliers," shows you how to apply various filters to get to both a long and short list of potential bidders.

Then Chapter 9, "Find the Right Solicitation Vehicle," describes different choices and schedules for diverse types of solicitation approaches, including RFIs, RFPs, and RFDs.

CHAPTER 7

Find More Than the Usual Suspects

If the business case for new or replacement technology has gotten validated and you've gleaned a decent understanding of your requirements (documented primarily in user stories), then you can begin to explore the broader solutions marketplace.

You'll want to carefully research just which type of technology will satisfy your needs, and what would constitute the broad set ("long list") of plausible suppliers. For information and research, be sure to cast a wide net and not rely on a single source of advice. Along the way, you may discover key bidders who weren't among your initial list of "usual suspects."

Also, you need to consider whether you should target software vendors (ISVs—independent software vendors)) or services firms (systems integrators, consultancies, or agencies) in your solicitation. It might make sense to issue two separate solicitations in sequence or a "combination" RFP that evaluates both the ISV and services partners together.

Which Marketplace?

What is a technology marketplace? It's an abstraction, really—a collection of competing tools that purport to do similar things in such a way that they attract a label, like "customer relationship management."

As with many abstractions, marketplace categories are part real, part ephemeral. Vendors sometimes get frustrated by such labels when they don't want to get pigeonholed ("We are so much more than a CRM package!"), but these categories are very useful for you. Labels simplify choices and give you a chance to compare solutions head to head.

Just remember that the categories aren't always as clean as the lines on a map. For example, marketplaces will usually overlap, which means that you can find similar capabilities in nominally different types of tools (see Figure 7.1).

The variations here can become fairly complex:

- One software platform can accomplish numerous needs that span separate marketplaces.

- Your business needs might span multiple marketplaces.

- Your requirements may fall somewhere "in-between," not precisely suited to any single category of tool.

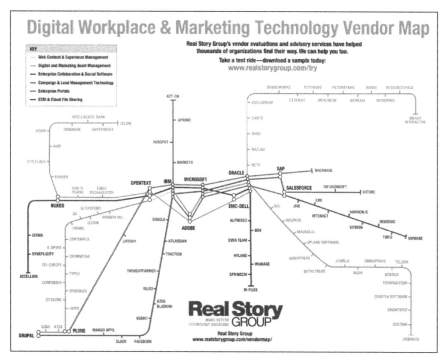

FIGURE 7.1

Like subway lines, technology marketplaces are distinct but connected and sometimes overlapping.

Analysis Paralysis

Consider the not-for-profit organization that assigned its CTO to lead a search for new digital asset management (DAM) technology. What started as a simple Google search quickly turned into a journey down a rabbit hole that ended with weeks of wasted time and a list of dozens of vendors.

When they brought us in to help, we quickly discovered that nearly three-quarters of the listed vendors were not even real DAM systems (even though the vendors called themselves DAMs.)

Simply putting parameters around what is and what is not a DAM sped up their process dramatically.

Lesson: Before creating lists of vendor possibilities, spend your initial research on determining which marketplace you should be exploring.

For the enterprise customer, the key to aligning with a specific marketplace is to look to your core. What is the most important piece of information or process related to your business case? If it's a customer record, then look to CRM services. If your core assets are videos, then look to media asset management platforms. Trying to automate an insurance claim? Then turn to BPM or workflow technologies. For more efficient invoice processing, you'll want to investigate the ERP or accounting software marketplaces.

CAUTION **OVER- AND UNDERESTIMATING AN INCUMBENT SOLUTION**

It's possible that your business needs could be satisfied by technology you already license, i.e., an "incumbent" solution.

The largest technology vendors like SAP, Microsoft, IBM, and Oracle promote their platforms as Swiss Army Knife–type environments that can stretch to fill multiple purposes. Your enterprise may see these as cornerstone investments and naturally want to gain maximum value here. But if using the incumbent vendor or platform means significantly less business value, then clearly you'll want to avoid this route.

The converse also sometimes happens: stakeholders deliberately eschew an incumbent solution because it has acquired a bad reputation internally. As often as not, this disrepute may stem from an implementation problem rather than a fundamental vendor or technology shortcoming.

In either case, you want to be fair to yourself and your supplier by giving incumbent vendors a chance to compete—*using the same test-based evaluation process that you'll apply to other challengers.* That way, you'll learn in an empirical way whether the incumbent player is really the right choice.

If you're not clear which category of technology will satisfy your needs, you should consider turning to outside advice (the next topic in this chapter).

The Enterprise That Discovered What They Really Needed

At Real Story Group we were called in to adjudicate an internal dispute at a major manufacturing company about whether they needed an enterprise portal platform or a digital asset management system to better serve their customers. In other words, which technology should they investigate?

Both technologies could plausibly add value by replacing a bevy of older, custom solutions. But when we dug deeper, we found that the biggest hurdles facing this firm were not technical. They were having trouble creating effective customer experiences in large part because they did not have authoritative master data sets around which to provide useful digital engagement.

Our advice to them? Hold off on pursuing either type of technology until they got their information house in order.

Lesson: Sometimes the best choice is no new technology at all.

Where to Get Good Information and Advice

Even in an era of unprecedented information sharing via social media, you will see extraordinary misinformation in the wild, and much of what passes for education comes from vendors themselves. That's not good. You will want to cast a wide (but critical) net and contrast various sources of advice.

Let's take a critical tour of possible information resources and their biases:

- Traditional analyst firms can identify major players, but suffer severe conflicts of interest, geographic blinders, and often dismiss open source and niche solutions.

- Consultancies can offer practical advice based on experience, but may not have a broad sense for the marketplaces, and integrators will tend to steer clients to favored tools.

- Industry associations provide useful meeting grounds but tend to cater to the needs of vendors who are their major underwriters.

- Vendor user groups can provide extraordinarily useful information and contacts, but typically it's just about a single vendor or product.

- Peer groups can offer excellent intelligence about relevant vendors and approaches, but you may not want to copycat industry competitors.

- Crowdsourced review sites offer useful anecdotes but tend to provide unduly generous reviews and lack evaluation structures for rigorous analysis.

- Vendors obviously offer a lot of information, most usefully actual product demos, where you can see tools in action, but are obviously biased.

Here's a short summary of pros and cons in Table 7.1.

TABLE 7.1 CONTRASTING SOURCES OF ADVICE

Advice Source	Pros	Cons	Use to...
Industry Peers	Information can be unusually candid, relevant	Tendency to "follow the herd"—may prove to be faddish	Sense-check your thinking and get ideas about lesser-known vendors
Consultancies and Systems Integrators	Deep knowledge of individual vendors can be valuable	May only know a subset of tools and tend to be biased toward partners	Learn about actual implementation costs and case studies in your industry segment
Industry Analysts	Have a broad understanding of the marketplace	Gross conflicts of interest skew their findings, in particular a tendency to over-promote large vendors	Get a sense for the larger players in the market
Crowd Review Sites	You can glean nuggets about what works well for different types of customers	Vendors tend to be scored very highly, technical considerations get underweighted, and absence of evaluation frameworks reduces value	Obtain some insights into topics to examine with specific suppliers
Trade Press	Frequently highlight case studies of technologies that have worked well	Coverage can be fawning and uncritical; difficult to glean patterns of vendor tendencies	See examples of what has worked with some other customers
Vendors	Can offer recorded or custom demos so you can see the tools in action	They are inherently biased toward their own solution and have a tendency to obfuscate	Get a general sense for how the technology could work in an idealized environment

Ideally, you will employ a combination of resources to build a composite picture of solutions marketplaces to understand better where you "fit," without excessively closing options at this stage. As a provider of vendor-neutral evaluation research, we're biased toward expert advice. But we're also frequently ashamed by the obsequiousness of some of our analyst brethren when it comes to evaluating vendors.

> **CAUTION** **FIVE SIGNS A VENDOR INFLUENCED AN ANALYST REPORT**
>
> Technology industry analyst reports can seem authoritative, but you need to beware of findings skewing in favor of suppliers over customers. How do you know when an assessment was written more for the vendor's interest than for you the customer? Here are five tells.
>
> 1. When the report employs euphemisms for product shortcomings.
>
>   Here's a dead give-away: when a report labels real weaknesses as "challenges."
>
> 2. When the report takes vendor promises uncritically.
>
>   Vendors will try to persuade analysts of a pending fix to any real shortcomings, but there's a good chance another kind of fix was already in.
>
> 3. When the report employs fake criticism.
>
>   Analysts avoid criticizing vendors by listing "challenges" that don't really matter to customers—like a perceived lack of marketing acumen.
>
> 4. When the report doesn't grade on a curve.
>
>   Typically, a vendor or technology needs to be writhing on its deathbed to receive a less-than-average rating in a traditional analyst report.
>
> 5. When the report avoids taboo topics.
>
>   In vendor-influenced reports, certain topics become taboo, so you rarely see criticisms of even ubiquitous problems like scalability, customer support, and ease-of-use.
>
> We encourage you to see through the fake gravitas that characterizes most analyst output. You're the one spending money on tools, so insist on candor and look for tough critiques, the true sign of objectivity.

So there are many conflicts of interest among potential advisors. But never fear, the methodology in this book will have you casting a wide net and employing your own eyes and fingertips to understand which solution is right for you. Put another way: do use research and advice to help steer you in the right direction, but depend on your own, test-based experience to dictate where you end up.

Which Type of Supplier: Tech Vendor Versus Services Firm?

As technologies become more complex, they can require more expertise to implement—expertise typically found in outside services from consultancies, integrators, and digital agencies. Depending on the type and size of the system you procure, you may spend 2–10× on consulting versus technology.

Given that ratio, does it make sense to focus more on the implementation partner than the technology vendor? We think not. Implementation partners come and go, but your choice of software will stick with you for a long, long time. Put another way: there are 60 ways to leave your services firm, but only one very unpleasant way to leave your tech vendor.

Whenever you start a technology project, get clear about what you need from any outside consultants. You may need various "soft skills," such as information and process analysis, user experience, and change management. Your software vendor's own professional services arm—which focuses narrowly on getting their technology implemented—won't prove very strong there.

Other times, though, you may only need specialized system implementation support and training based on clear specifications you've already developed, in which case a broad-scale consulting firm would present a poor fit, and you might want to simply rely on the vendor's services organization.

Vendor services organizations and outside consultancy/integrators both have their pros and cons. Consider using either (or both) depending on your own specific needs.

TABLE 7.2 COMPARING VENDOR VERSUS PARTNER SERVICES

	Outside Services Firm	Vendor Services Organization
Key Skills	Specifications, info and process analysis, systems integration	Rapid tool implementation
Scope	Often sees the big picture but may lack specific tool expertise	Knows the tool, but may not see the bigger picture
Focus	Will want to focus on long-term fit and subsequent projects	Will want to get to launch quickly and then leave
Resources	Can likely staff up and across, to scale with your needs, but can prove people-heavy	Can supply talent on a flexible basis, but day rates will run higher
Duration	Tends toward long embrace	Prefers hit and run

CONCLUSION: If you need strategic and requirements advice, including business case support, go with an outside services firm.

If you decide you need an integration or implementation partner, the question remains, which do you pick first: vendor or partner? You could pick the services partner first and let them bring in the tool they think is best. We tend to recommend this only if you are looking to implement several major packaged solutions simultaneously and need a general contractor to prove how they can piece together all the right parts. For most customers seeking a single type of technology, though, this represents a high-risk approach for all but the smallest projects. Integrators will naturally tend to steer you toward the more limited set of tools they know (or have a vested interest in).

Any assessment of long-term risks and rewards has to look at switching costs. Replacing a consultant or integrator is certainly painful, but at the end of the day, it's tougher to leave your software vendor. Your content and data are structured for their repository. Your templates, workflows, and other customizations are tied to their system. Your customizations and extensions to the platform are tied to their API.

If changing integrators is like switching plumbers, then changing vendors is like remodeling your bathroom completely. Get a blueprint, select the fixtures, and *then* find the plumber.

CAUTION **BEWARE CONSULTINGWARE**

Services firms—especially systems integrators—write a lot of code. That code can serve multiple purposes, from customizing a software package to integrating two systems to creating entirely new features from scratch. In the last case, services firms sometimes seek to reuse that code base with other clients.

In other cases, the services firm will want to package up the code and sell it as actual software or a cloud service. This is how some software companies start, so it's a known strategy, but you the customer need to be aware that a services firm may not have the right chops to actually support true software. Real software requires things that most services firms eschew:

- Formalized customer support (ideally 24/7/365)

- A significant investment in code "abstraction" so that the software can be used across multiple types of customers, and not just some anchor clients

- A structured roadmap of major and minor improvements, which requires developers and others who are not committed to consulting projects

- An ecosystem of other services firms who can implement the solution, some of whom might compete with the originating firm

In short, delivering a service and delivering a product are two different things. Services firms typically make poor software product companies unless they totally commit to changing their skin.

In an ideal world, you would pick the software vendor first and then have a second round of competition for a services partner or two. We have mentored and counseled many enterprises in this approach, and it works well. The downside is that it takes more time and effort up front, even if it pays off in the long run. See Chapter 17, "Adapt This Process for Selecting Services Firms," on how to run a separate solicitation for a services firm.

For those on a faster track, we sometimes recommend a "combination" RFP. In this approach, you ask the technology vendor and services partner to bid together, and you evaluate them together.

You do face some complications with this approach, but in our experience, it can work pretty well.

A "combination" selection approach can also yield other benefits. First, this approach is more amenable to cloud-based providers, who typically promote an integrated technology+services model that might not fit neatly into solicitations targeting just technology or only services. It also provides more opportunities to clearly evaluate open source platforms, where you often need to engage a third-party integrator to fully understand the platform.

In the appendix, "Resources and Examples," we include sample RFPs for both a software procurement and an interactive agency solicitation.

Tips

- Explore whether your enterprise already owns the technology that could meet your needs, but never default to the incumbent supplier.

- Take a long look at any software category before committing to it, and consider other "adjacent" technology segments that might also meet your needs.

- Obtain advice from a variety of sources, but understand the limitations and biases of each.

- Get clear about the ecosystem around any technology segment, and begin to plot out where and how you will obtain implementation and other services support.

- An ideal approach has you selecting the software first, then the services partner, but both through a competitive process.

- Avoid "consultingware" and look for true software suppliers in order to maximize your chances for long-term success.

CHAPTER 8

How to Target the Right Suppliers

ow that you have a decent understanding of a particular technology marketplace, it's time to identify those suppliers that may potentially meet your needs. Initially, you'll want to explore as wide a set of potential suppliers as possible, to give yourself the best odds of finding an optimal solution. This is a process of getting to a "long list" first and then a "short list" of vendors to approach, as shown in Figure 8.1.

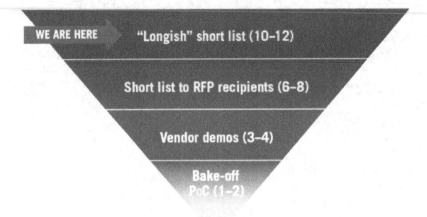

SELECTION (1)

FIGURE 8.1
Your first goal in targeting suppliers is to develop a "long list."

Various filtering criteria can help get you to a good long list. From there, the most important differentiators will revolve around a scenario "fit" of a particular vendor.

Use the Right Filtering Criteria for a Long List

Initially, you should consider some basic filters when looking at the marketplace, in order to get to a "long list" of perhaps as many as 10 to 12 vendors. In rough order of priority (see Figure 8.2), use these filters:

1. **Regions:** Does the vendor have a decent customer/partner/support footprint in your region or country?

2. **Delivery Models:** Does the vendor's orientation toward a cloud match with yours?

3. **Licensing Models:** How is the product costed out, and what are the implications for your budget?

4. **Technologies:** What specific technical skills are required to configure and extend the platform, and do they match with what you can muster?

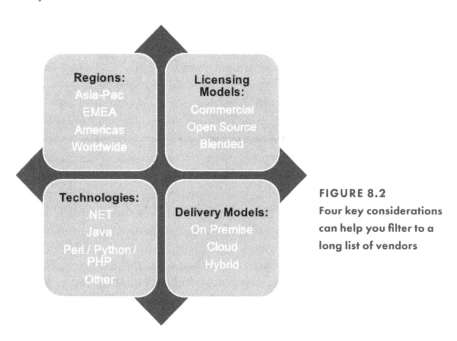

FIGURE 8.2
Four key considerations can help you filter to a long list of vendors

While these basic criteria are important, don't be too rigid at this phase in making them absolute discriminators. Resist the temptation to dramatically narrow down what should be a large initial capture list. For example, even if your enterprise has only Java developers internally, you probably still don't want to rule out non-Java solutions entirely. If the business fit is ideal, you might be able to find the right Java skills.

Once you get beyond core attributes, you'll want to explore vendor "tiers." Vendors tend to cluster based on various criteria, including size and complexity. In our experience, complexity is the most meaningful criterion, as it usually relates to overall cost, level of effort, and potential value from your investment (see Figure 8.3).

Products vs. Platforms

<u>Platforms</u>: Developers can make custom applications
<u>Products</u>: They do certain things well right away

Typically Platform Oriented	Typically Product Oriented
IT Leadership: We can meet future demands	Business Users: It works today
Senior Management: We can cover multiple use cases with one investment	Line employees: Just solve my problem
Systems Integrators: We can accomplish whatever the client asks	End-user Companies: Keep it cheap, easy & fast

Platforms   Costly   **Products**
Functionally Rich

⟵————————————————————⟶

Complex
More   Time to Deploy   **Less**

FIGURE 8.3

Most software falls on a spectrum from highly malleable platforms to very straightforward products.

The location of a particular vendor offering on the platform-product continuum will play a significant role in how well the solution fits your short- and long-term needs. Product-oriented tools tend to trade short-term wins for long-term inflexibility, while platforms tend to offer greater long-term opportunity in exchange for higher resource requirements. Platforms demo better; products launch faster. Platforms require more (and more constant) technical attention; products mean that sometimes you can't achieve a particular goal, regardless of the resources you throw at it. Most open source projects lean in the platform direction. Most SaaS offerings are more product-like.

People have biases here. We tend to lean toward the product side of the spectrum, having seen enterprises struggle with platform-oriented tools as their overstretched staff failed to get full value out of them. Other advisors may argue for a more platform-oriented approach, and your organization's leadership may get pitched to consolidate to fewer strategic vendor relationships.

There's no solid right or wrong here, but consider the following information (see Figure 8.4):

- Clarify whether your **business case calls for short-term ROI versus long-term capacity building**. Products typically offer the former at the expense of the latter. It's hard to achieve both from the same software.

- Similarly, when selecting vendors, have the **difficult internal conversation about present needs versus future flexibility**. Do this early in the process, or you'll be fighting it out later via vendor proxies.

- **Take a hard look at your internal capabilities and program-level maturity.** If you can boast comparatively advanced internal resources and experience, you could obtain a real competitive advantage by going with a platform rather than a product. If you're running lean, then admit that you can't address the complexity that comes with exploiting all that extra power and consider more productized solutions.

RSG VENDOR EVALUATIONS

Enterprise Collaboration & Social Networking Logo Landscape

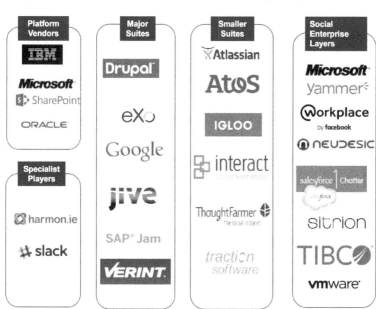

FIGURE 8.4

The marketplace for enterprise social-collaboration technology circa 2017 spans (left to right) from platforms to products.

As you assemble a "long list," you'll want to identify roughly in what tier you belong. Better yet, figure out what multiple tiers you might span. Are you looking mostly at platforms? Include a couple products just to make sure you couldn't get away with something simpler, and vice-versa.

CAUTION **BIGGER IS NOT ALWAYS BETTER**

When we were in our younger days in the enterprise technology industry, we noticed that some of the best solutions came from smaller vendors. Upon hearing this, our elders would pull us aside and say, "Sure, but how much longer will that vendor be around?" That's a hard argument to counter, because, of course, everyone harbors fears about their vendors' viability, and who wants to get stuck with an unsupported product?

Two decades and much gray hair later, we've come to the conclusion that the biggest vendors can actually carry the highest risks in terms of product continuity. IBM, Microsoft, Oracle, EMC, Google, and SAP aren't going to fail as companies, but they will kill individual products at the drop of a hat. Remember, they are constantly buying other vendors, and their own product strategies will shift quickly, due to market shifts or investment pressure, to which the biggest players are especially susceptible.

Smaller vendors, especially those focused on one tool, stake their corporate lives on their offering. Their product could still weaken over time—and as a customer, you need to stay on top of innovation and support levels—but you typically won't see a capricious decision to discontinue it outright.

Could your small, focused vendor go kaput? Sure. Can open source projects wither? Absolutely. Look at viability and continuity as a multidimensional risk factor. In the end, though, if stability is a high priority, the biggest vendors may not present your best choice.

If you take an RFI-based approach (see Chapter 9, "Find the Right Solution Vehicle") as opposed to an RFP/tender-based approach, you might send the RFI to this complete long list. For an RFP, though, you'll want to filter down to a narrower, "short list."

Use Scenario Analysis to Get to Short Lists

Explicitly or not, different tools target different use cases. Any technology platform or product "wants" to behave a certain way. Vendors will boast about omnibus capabilities, but baked in underneath is a vision about how a particular subset of problems gets solved. This reflects a kind of imprinting: the tool's initial incubators or flagship customers wanted it for those specific use cases. The product might have broadened its scope as it matured, but typically the initial roots remain visible.

The key for you is to match a vendor's sweet-spot use cases with your specific needs, and the way to do this is via scenario analysis. Think of a scenario as a high-level business use case, like "peer-based customer support" for customer relationship management systems, or "short-form video" for media asset management technology. Note that these are business uses, and not technical attributes.

How a product's fundamental scenario fit aligns with your intended use cases should be *the primary filter* when determining your initial short list of vendors to evaluate.

Understanding the business scenarios that fit better or worse for the different packages enables you to see deeper into their relative strengths and weaknesses *for your particular circumstances*. Let's look at two examples, where a customer is looking to create a short list around enterprise portal technology (see Figures 8.5 and 8.6).

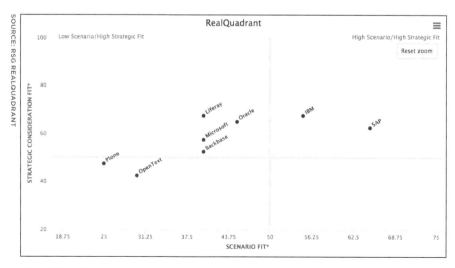

FIGURE 8.5

In this first quadrant, the customer emphasizes integration and self-support scenarios.

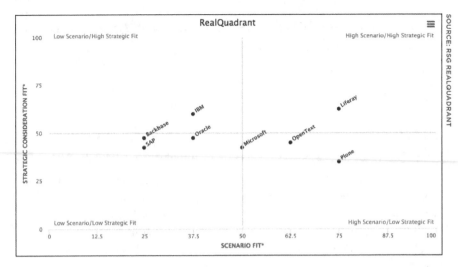

FIGURE 8.6

In this quadrant, the customer emphasized content aggregation scenarios (and lower cost), and came up with a different set of top vendors to target.

It is important to understand how vertically specialized the marketplace you are investigating tends to be. In some software marketplaces, functional use-case scenarios can trump vertical industry specialization and expertise. In other marketplaces, we recommend considering vertical expertise as scenarios themselves. In these cases, you should weigh vertical scenarios side-by-side with functional scenarios.

Consider these canonical scenarios from two differing marketplaces, where functional use cases are paramount in enterprise social-collaboration technology, while vertical expertise should be considered alongside functional scenarios in the digital and media asset management marketplace.

Enterprise Social-Collaboration Technology

Marketing objective:

- B2B lead management and nurturing
- B2C lead management and offers
- Social customer support and engagement
- Social media intelligence
- Social media monitoring

Marketing channel emphasis:

- Mobile marketing
- Social marketing campaigns

Digital and Media Asset Management

Vertical expertise:

- Advertising and creative agencies
- Fast-moving consumer goods
- Government
- Manufacturing
- Media and entertainment
- Nonprofit, education, and heritage
- Pharmaceutical, healthcare, and medical
- Retail and ecommerce

Image and brand management:

- Advertising and marketing asset management
- Basic brand management
- DAM library or photo archive
- Multilingual brand management

Publishing:

- Multichannel publishing
- Periodical and catalog production and management

Corporate time-based media management:

- Audio and video library review and approval
- Audio and video production and reuse
- Broadcast media management

How short should you make your short list? Your short list doesn't need to be *too short*. As we'll see later, if you target six to eight vendors for an RFP, there's a good chance only two to six will respond with proposals. Why is that? Well, we've found on average that even the best RFPs from the biggest customers see a 33–66% response rate.

You'll see in the next few chapters that there are various things you can do to improve that rate, but the overall lesson here is that you should cast a wide net at this point. The only exception: if you are *certain* that a particular vendor will never win your business, ethics dictate that you should not invite them to participate, just because you are curious or want to increase the overall competitive energy.

On the other hand, in some situations, you may find that only two or three suppliers can meet your criteria. This can happen in niche marketplaces, or when you have unusually stringent (and fixed) constraints. In that case, you may want to explore doing an abbreviated "request for demo" (RFD) approach. Or alternatively, if you can't agree on a short list of as few as eight suppliers, then you'll want to pursue a "request for information" (RFI) approach. That's the subject of the next chapter.

CAUTION BE WARY OF THE "HOT" VENDOR

There's definitely a "bandwagon" effect in technology, particularly around digital tools. Certain products get "hot" and attract an outsized following based in part on a cool reputation. Be careful before jumping on any bandwagons, because often the hottest vendors and open source projects are where customers can experience the most heartburn.

There are many reasons for this:

- Vendor management gets distracted, by media requests, analyst relations, raising money while they're still hot, or appeasing investors

- Rapid expansion leads to hiring people who don't actually know much about that platform

- Their partner consulting channel gets similarly strained, overcommitted, and on aggregate, underexperienced

- Your own internal staff who learn the platform's innards get recruited away by headhunters

To be sure, you can see similar problems occur in a vendor experiencing the opposite—a death spiral. Those are quite rare, but definitely painful. In the long term, a successful vendor should in theory figure out how to garner resources to address its growing pains. That may be small comfort to you in the near term—and you need to show results in the near term. Make sure that your selection process focuses on actual vendor performance and not reputation.

Tips

- The ideal long list is between 8 to 12 vendors; use basic filtering criteria (e.g., geographic footprint) to develop this list.

- The ideal short list is between 6 to 8 vendors; focus on your use cases to filter this list.

- Don't lock into a single "tier" of vendors (e.g., high-end, lower-end) at this point.

- Remember that typically only 33–66% of your short-list vendors will respond to your RFP, so cast a wide net.

- To that end, don't just focus on recognizable, "name" vendors.

- Do not place a vendor on your list if you are certain it would not constitute a good fit—it's a waste of your time *and* the vendor's time.

CHAPTER 9

Find the Right Solicitation Vehicle

There are multiple solicitation approaches that you can use to engage vendors. An RFP (request for proposal)—sometimes known as a *tender*—formally solicits potential suppliers to propose solutions for your needs.

You may want to consider issuing an RFI (request for information) prior to an RFP, if your earlier analysis suggests a lack of readiness to implement a solution, or if you believe you need more education on the technologies and marketplace. In rare cases, you may want to issue a simple RFQ (request for quote) to solicit pricing information or to confirm broad cost ranges if you are still seeking budget approval.

You'll also need to invest the time and effort into this process commensurate with the criticality of the technology you're selecting. So, in some cases, you'll want to take some shortcuts. For example, you can employ an RFD (request for demo) in cases where your target list is small and you want to save the time by skipping directly to the demo phase. In any event, it's important to set a realistic schedule, for yourself as well as your bidders.

RFI vs. RFP/Tender vs. RFQ

First, you should decide which route is best to pursue:

- Request for information

- Request for proposal/tender

- Request for quote

Note that these three approaches are *not* mutually exclusive. An RFI typically precedes an RFP, with bidder replies informing your solicitation. You can embed some components of an RFQ into any solicitation where you request pricing.

Still, they are different approaches, so let's summarize them in Table 9.1.

If you follow the adaptive methodology in this book, you may not need to issue an RFI and instead go straight to an RFP that includes an RFQ component. Still we wish that more customers went with RFIs, especially in particularly tricky environments where you seek multiple technologies at once, or you think your requirements remain too fuzzy. The major trade-off is that you may expend 6 to 12 weeks issuing the document, giving vendors time to respond, and then assessing the written replies.

TABLE 9.1 COMPARING SOLICITATION TYPES

	RFI	RFP	RFQ
Core Purpose	Learn more	Vet vendors	Compare costs
Use When	You need more clarity on the marketplace and what the tools can and can't really do.	When you have a short list of plausible vendors and want them to propose how they can best fit your specific needs.	You have a very precise set of quantifiable specifications, or you simply want to understand potential costs better.
Pros	You can learn more about what's possible with different technologies and vendors. You can produce a substantially higher-quality RFP.	Enables vendors to compete head-to-head against your specific requirements. Conveys a sense of seriousness and immediacy that encourages bidders to participate.	Enables you to get exact pricing on something very specific and tangible, like hardware. Helps you build a reasonable budget before you go out with a formal RFP.
Cons	Adds time and effort to your process. Vendors may not respond or put in full effort if you don't have an actual funded project yet.	You may learn some unexpected but important information about your needs or the market that requires you to "reset" the process.	Doesn't give you a complete sense of value on more intangible goods and services like software and implementation. Vendors may not participate in what they perceive as a commodity-pricing exercise.

To the extent that many digital initiatives require consulting work—at least for the initial implementation—consider sending any RFI to systems integrators or other consultancies in addition to software vendors. You will get varying responses from services firms, and they may not help you narrow your shortlist. However, you can learn from their suggestions, and it may crystallize whether the RFP should ultimately go out to vendors or integrators.

The Association That Learned Through an RFI

We worked with a major medical professional association that ran a complicated certification process for a particular set of medical professionals, entailing large sets of paper files, emails, spreadsheets, and PDFs. They wanted to know the best way to digitize the whole operation, and had a lot of questions, which they rolled up into an RFI:

- What kind of software was needed? They had been exploring enterprise content management (ECM), business process management (BPM), workflow, and eLearning marketplaces.

- How long would the implementation take, and what were their migration options and associated costs?

- How broadly available was the expertise in their particular industry and use cases?

- How complex were the tools to use, and what was the attendant training and education effort they should anticipate for the association administrative staff?

The association cast a wide net for the RFI, including to some systems integrators with experience in this area. They learned that the type of technology they were seeking was "case management" software, and that the target vendor list would likely differ based on whether their approach would turn out to be content-centric or process-centric. They learned that several vendors and integrators had specific expertise with association-based certification systems. And they learned that the implementation was best concluded as a series of steps rather than a total cut-over.

The association then re-examined its specific requirements and confidently went out to a final short list with a highly targeted RFP.

Lesson: RFIs can help you significantly clarify your needs and opportunities.

Set a Realistic Schedule

Finding the right fit takes time and effort. Just how much time and effort should depend on the criticality of that solution to your enterprise.

- If you are a retailer selecting a new ecommerce platform, you will want to spend as much as six months to a year on the effort, since the consequences could make or break your business

- If you are a mid-sized manufacturing company looking to improve internal collaboration among your desk-bound knowledge workers, you'll want to spend no more than two to four months on the process

Consider these two schedules in Table 9.2. Both are reasonable, but the "long" schedule is more suited to a more complex and business-critical digital offering. The short version still goes through all the steps, but gives you and the vendor less time to complete them. This works only when you are procuring something simpler and less business-intensive, or when the risks of making a poor choice are lower.

TABLE 9.2 COMPARING A LONG VERSUS SHORT SCHEDULE

Step	Long (Weeks)	Short (Weeks)
Draft RFP	2–4	1–2
Determine vendor short list	1–2	0–1
Obtain NDAs and issue RFP	1–2	0–1
Vendors prep and deliver proposals	4–6	3–4
Team evaluates and downselects	2–3	1–2
Vendor short list preps for demos	2–3	1–2
Demo week	1	1
Downselect to two finalists	1–2	0–1
Vendors prep for PoC	3–5	2–3
Conduct two hands-on PoCs	2–4	1–2
Decide on winner	1–2	0–1
Total time (weeks)	20–34	10–20

Don't worry so much about the individual rows; we'll explain them in more detail later in Parts IV, "Engage with Suppliers," and V, "Try Before You Buy." Also, your timing may differ depending on things as diverse as team coherence to vendor availability to holiday schedules. Instead, focus the mind on the total times at the bottom and set your colleagues' expectations accordingly.

Of course, you need to communicate a schedule to your vendor. Here's an example in Table 9.3 from a hypothetical "short" selection schedule for an RFP.

TABLE 9.3 HYPOTHETICAL SHORT SCHEDULE

Activity	Date
RFP release date	April 30
Intent to respond	May 7
Last day for bidder questions	May 10
RFP closing date and submission deadline	May 28
Internal review of proposals	Week of June 4
Notification of short-listed vendors	June 8
Vendor demo week	Week of June 18
Selection of two finalists	June 25
Proof-of-concept prep	Weeks of June 25–July 2
PoC with finalist one	Week of July 9
PoC with finalist two	Week of July 23
Final decision	Early August

Note that the selection team needs be organized and decisive to hit those milestones, so before you embed this in your RFP, make sure that everyone signs off on it.

SIGNING THE CONTRACT MAY BECOME THE BIGGEST HOLD-UP

The biggest delays in the entire selection process may well come from your own enterprise: how quickly can you make decisions, especially around filtering out vendors as you go through this iterative process.

But there's one other very common hold-up: signing the contract(s) once you've settled on a finalist. This sometimes stems from bureaucratic inertia, but often reflects the complexity of final clarification and negotiation over terms and pricing. There are two things you can do to avoid long delays:

- Insist on sample contracts as part of the proposal process and start negotiating terms and pricing as you winnow down the bidder list (see Chapter 15, "Negotiate Like a Pro").

- Include a procurement or contracts specialist on the selection team so that person is up to speed and can move faster once a decision is made.

Above all, you need to plan realistically for this critical milestone as you schedule out the transition from technology acquisition to initial implementation.

Possible Shortcut Process

Sometimes, you may want to (or need to) abbreviate the full process described earlier for any of the following reasons:

- Your time frame is compressed.

- You have a limited set of target vendors.

- You want to overweight the process toward hands-on testing rather than reading proposals.

If any of these events occurs, you can follow an abbreviated process that we'll call "request for demo" or RFD.

With an RFD, you "grandfather" three to five bidders to the demo round. Note, however, that you still want written proposals from them, to see diagrams, references, pricing, terms, and such. (Sometimes, we'll even call these an RFP&D—request for proposal and demo.) It's just that you won't use those proposals as a filtering mechanism, and bidders can deliver them just before the demo round. Typically, you don't ask them to give narrative answers to the scenarios in your RFD either, since they're going to demo those for you.

If time is even tighter, or you know that the short list consists of only two vendors, then you could go straight to PoC (again with written proposals from the bidders). We rarely counsel this, but have seen it work well in the right circumstances.

Consider this short analysis of trade-offs among the three options (see Figure 9.1).

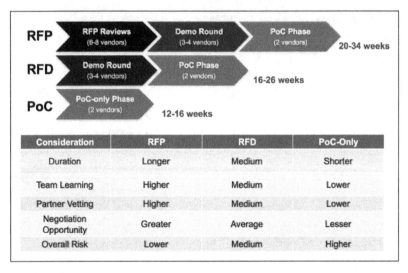

Consideration	RFP	RFD	PoC-Only
Duration	Longer	Medium	Shorter
Team Learning	Higher	Medium	Lower
Partner Vetting	Higher	Medium	Lower
Negotiation Opportunity	Greater	Average	Lesser
Overall Risk	Lower	Medium	Higher

FIGURE 9.1

Contrasting three different approaches to vetting a potential bidder list.

We encourage enterprise buyers to go the RFP route whenever possible. It offers the greatest degree of team learning (which bodes well for the future implementation) and maximizes your negotiation leverage. An RFP process also mitigates against the risk of poor choices, missed opportunities, or outright selection failure. If you start with two vendors in a PoC, what happens if neither works out?

That said, there is no perfect approach. You need to balance time and effort against expected return and the criticality of the solution you're procuring.

CAUTION BEWARE THE CANNED RFP

Sometimes, vendors or marketplace consultants will give you canned RFPs under the guise of a time-saver. These aren't templates like the kind you'll find in this book's appendix, "Resources and Examples," mind you; they're pre-made, ready-to-go RFPs where you just insert your company name and a few details.

Don't use them.

Every other vendor has seen them and—presuming the project is hardwired for a competitor—will not participate. In addition to being very busy, technology vendors are also very suspicious. So if your field of competition is truly open—and it should be—don't suggest otherwise by starting with a canned template. Instead, challenge vendors with real narratives (see Chapter 10, "Create RFPs That Actually Work") and use your own requirements under your authentic voice to find your best solution.

Tips

- For a very large digital initiative, consider an RFI to educate your team, and clarify opportunities and costs before issuing an RFP.

- RFQs typically only make sense when you are selecting more commoditized products and services (rarely the case in digital initiatives).

- Set a realistic schedule that allows for iteration and adaptation in your process.

- Allocate time and resources in proportion to the criticality of this technology to your overall business success.

- An RFD can save you time, but may yield reduced business benefits and higher risks.

- Going straight to RFD places an even greater premium on getting the right short list.

- If you elect the RFD route, you should still require bidders to submit a written response, including a financial proposal (consider calling it an RFP&D).

- Remember that the biggest potential hold-up may prove to be financial and contractual wrangling; plan to start this early in the process.

- Consider reviewing RFP templates to jump-start your process, but never issue a fully canned RFP written by a vendor.

PART IV

Engage with Suppliers

Now comes the time to engage with suppliers in a structured process that includes issuing RFPs, handling Q&A, and evaluating written proposals.

RFPs have a bad reputation for good reason. Too often, they fail to clarify what the issuer truly needs, and instead force bidders to jump through extraneous hoops. The problem is not the process itself, but the enterprises that fail to develop *effective* RFPs.

Chapter 10, "Create RFPs That Actually Work," shows you how to craft effective RFPs. What should you be sure to ask? What is superfluous or counterproductive? How can an RFP help you screen for usability and "fit?" What's the best way to request normalized pricing on bids? It will conclude with pitfalls to avoid, such as long checklists and unstructured pricing guidelines.

Bidders will have questions and feedback, and this interaction can be useful for both parties—as long as you conduct a formal and fair process here. Chapter 11, "Keeping It Real with Bidders," shows you how to do just that.

Then you'll receive actual proposals and the real vetting begins. Chapter 12, "How to Evaluate Proposals Critically," offers advice on how to assess vendor proposals.

CHAPTER 10

Create RFPs That Actually Work

An effective RFP goes a long way toward attracting an effective, substantive response from suppliers. An RFP (or RFI or RFD) has several key parts. First, you want to introduce your enterprise and the business problem you are trying to solve. Second, the core of your RFP should lie with your scenarios, followed by technical and business questions. Third, you need to obtain key vendor and pricing information in a structured way. Finally, you must be very clear about the schedule and process for selection.

Your RFP Outline

Let's look at the major sections of an RFP in Figures 10.1 and 10.2 and the descriptions below.

1. **Purpose:** Where you offer a summary, describe and delimit the program scope, and where possible, describe the ideal supplier.

2. **Organizational Overview:** Where you describe your organization and also any incumbent systems or processes (with metrics) that you are replacing, and why, plus any future-state planning you've done.

3. **Program Scope and Plan:** Where you identify the scope of this effort and explain your selection plan.

4. **Business Scenarios:** Where you describe to-be narrative actions by key personas (which you'll learn about later in this chapter).

5. **Advanced Q&A:** Where you ask specific questions about fit in terms of integration, functional, system, and implementation services, as well as infrastructure compatibility, where relevant (more about this later in Chapter 11, "Keeping It Real with Bidders").

6. **Written Submission Outline:** Where you describe how the vendor's proposal should be structured, and where you ask for their approach to things like architecture, support, and training, as well as ask for references, pricing, and sample contracts.

7. **Selection Process and Schedule:** Where you outline the overall selection schedule, as well as detail the demo-day(s) and PoC agendas.

1. Purpose of this RFP 4
   1.1 Summary 4
   1.2 Business Objectives for New CMS Platform 4

2. Organizational Overview 6
   2.1 About University University 6
   2.2 Our Key Properties 6
   2.3 Operational Background 6
   2.4 Key Metrics 6

3. Program Scope and Plan 8
   3.1 Scope 8
   3.2 Selection Plan 8
   3.3 Implementation plan 8

4. Business Scenarios 10
   4.1 Structure 10
   4.2 Scenarios 10
      4.2.1 Scenario 1: Creating a new page 10
      4.2.2 Scenario 2: Creating a new microsite 11
      4.2.3 Scenario 3: Managing and using media assets 12
      4.2.4 Scenario 4: Student contributor, with approval process 14
      4.2.5 Scenario 5: Modifying Template to include related items 15
      4.2.6 Scenario 6: Create new content type with date-based display 16
      4.2.7 Scenario 7: Emergency Publish 16

5. Advanced Q&A 18
   5.1 Integration Services 18
      5.1.1 Google Analytics 18
      5.1.2 Google AdWords 18
      5.1.3 ExactTarget 18
      5.1.4 JavaScript Widgets 19
      5.1.5 WordPress 19
      5.1.6 YouTube 19
      5.1.7 Active Directory and System Entitlements 19
      5.1.8 Enterprise Applications 20
   5.2 Functional Services 20
      5.2.1 Taxonomy Management Services 20
      5.2.2 Friendly URLs 20
      5.2.3 Mobile Services 20
      5.2.4 Forms Services 21
   5.3 System Services 21
      5.3.1 External Site Security 21
      5.3.2 Disaster Recovery 21
   5.4 Infrastructure compatibility 21

FIGURE 10.1
The first part of the RFP should talk about who you are and what you need.

6. Written Submission Outline 23
   6.1 Executive Summary 23
   6.2 System architectural design 23
   6.3 Completed Responses to Business Scenarios and Advanced Q&A 23
   6.4 Proposed approach to maintenance and support 23
   6.5 Proposed approach to PoC 23
   6.6 Training 23
   6.7 Background about your company and solution 23
      6.7.1 Corporate profile 23
      6.7.2 System Releases 24
      6.7.3 Financial viability 24
      6.7.4 References 24
   6.8 Costs and charges 24
      6.8.1 PoC Firm Fixed price 25
   6.9 Sample Contracts 25
   6.10 Appendices 25

7. Selection Process and Schedule 26
   7.1 Schedule of events 26
   7.2 Agenda for full-day demo meetings 28
   7.3 PoC Process 29
   7.4 Cancellation of request 29

FIGURE 10.2
The second part of the RFP should dictate the proposal format, including information about the vendor and their pricing, as well as the overall schedule.

Anatomy of an Effective User Story

Your user stories should comprise the meat of the document, so spend time here to get them right. (You may need some external help here.) Stories are based on key personas, so you'll want to make sure you've cataloged those first. The narrative describes what those personas do in an idealized future environment. Note that the narrative should be descriptive, not prescriptive. *Don't* ask the vendor to show "a green submit button in the upper left." *Do* describe what you want to happen in general terms and let them prescribe the right approach.

Here are the pieces that make up an effective user story:

1. **Name:** A shorthand reference.

2. **User Profiles:** The roles, e.g., contact center rep, or first-time customer.

3. **Personas:** The actors' names, etc. Connie the rep, or Cassius the customer.

4. **Description:** One-sentence summary of what you are trying to do.

5. **Background:** A paragraph or several offering context on the personas and the particular business environment for this persona.

6. **Objective:** One or two sentences cueing in the bidder on exactly what business goal you are trying to achieve.

7. **Narrative:** What the personas actually do (see Real Story sidebar on pp. 98–99).

8. **Optional Variant:** A way to insert alternative endings or less important capabilities that the bidder can address in the demos only as time allows.

Note that if you are pursuing an RFD approach where all the bidders get grandfathered into the demo round, you should still include the scenarios (vendors will have to demo them), but obviate the need to provide written responses to them, which saves them time and allows you to compress the schedule a bit.

Finally, remember that the scenarios don't have to be perfect at this phase. You'll have a chance to refine and supplement them in subsequent demo and PoC rounds.

Vague RFPs only beget wordy responses that fail to adequately clarify your choices. Help your enterprise by removing conveniently ambiguous buzzwords. Here are three examples.

- **"Integrate":** This word allows you and the vendor to conspire in postponing discussion of the hard work coming your way. Instead of vaguely asking whether two systems can integrate, devise actual test cases. Articulate specific needs for read- or write-access to repositories, as well as event-triggers. Describe key customer or employee experiences as they complete tasks that span multiple systems.

- **"Intuitive":** Intuitive to whom? Vendors are proud of their tools and always deem them easy to use, yet many customers report significant usability problems. True usability means *fitness to purpose*. Therefore, you need to discover your colleagues' and customers' true purposes in employing any tool.

- **"Robust":** This is a useless marketing term typically employed by vendors and their analyst shills. What most people mean here is "richly capable." That sounds like a good thing, but richness brings complexity, so if you mean "multifunctional," or "extensible," you may mitigate against the usability we were just seeking. Get clear about the functionality you seek and try not to buy any more than you need, since "robustness" always comes with a cost.

An Example RFP Narrative User Story

What does a user story narrative look like? Here's a short example from a digital asset management tender. See the example RFP in the appendix, "Resources and Examples," for more examples.

> Martha Marketing logs into the DAM system and sees a folder hierarchy, organized by product line; each product line contains subfolders with appropriate images or collateral. Each day, she uploads any new product photos and puts them into the appropriate directory. The system adds basic metadata to each, describing when it was uploaded, along with other basic file information. When Martha works on an image, she adds a description to each image, and from the set of drop-down menus, she selects different available resolutions for rendition-ing and makes multiple selections to indicate in which product groups it belongs.

> Don Distributor logs on to the DAM system via a web browser, but he can see only those folders for the product line that he sells and only the photos and collateral within those folders. Dan selects and drags all the product images and collateral he needs to a collection cart. When ready, he downloads all of them via a single ZIP file.

> Since he needs a special image, Don runs a query to see if the system has it. He finds what he's looking for and (with suitable permissions) downloads it. Don then creates new images using the built-in transformation tool, selecting the proper parameters or image name from a list, and the system generates a new image of that size, which he downloads to his desktop. When a subsequent search yields nothing, Don

How Vendors May Respond

Will some vendors find this RFP format prohibitively complex to respond to? Perhaps, although most will prefer its organized struc-ture. In our experience, a user story–based RFP tends to beget more targeted and relevant vendor responses, albeit potentially fewer in number. The test-based nature of a user story–based approach makes it easier to discriminate among them, which in turn leads to less contentious downselect meetings. When you're clearer about sends a request through the system to Martha for a special rendition of the image.

On Friday afternoon, Martha runs a weekly report to see which images have been used most, as well as to see which distributors are using the system and which are not, telling her which products the distributors are promoting most frequently.

With this use case, you have communicated several key points to the DAM vendor:

- You want to be more efficient in serving your distributors' marketing needs.

- You want to empower the distributors with a self-service collateral distribution system.

- You care about security and want the system to help control access to images.

- You want to free up Martha's time so that she can work more effectively with the distributors.

- You want reporting that gives you real business insight into asset usage.

But best of all, instead of listing all those as line-item "requirements," you get to see them in action by simulating real live actors in any future system.

Lesson: Always keep it real by making user stories the center of your selection process.

what you want and bidders have to be more specific about their real capabilities and tendencies, decisions come more easily.

Also, don't dismiss vendors' unwillingness to jump through the hoops of responding to a user story–based RFP. If they are unwilling to put in a bit more effort during the RFP response phase of this process, it's probably a good indicator of how they will react in the future when you ask for custom treatment (and you will ask for custom treatment at some point!).

Tips

- Avoid overly long and detailed technical requirements that dwarf clear business requirements.

- Be flexible enough for suppliers to provide creative solutions to your problems.

- Give vendors a reasonable time frame to respond (at least four to six weeks).

- Allow vendors to ask questions in writing (on a specific deadline).

- Make clear in word and deed that the RFP is not "hard-wired" for any single bidder.

- Be sure to preview that you will follow a test-based selection process, including a competitive PoC.

- Treat prospective bidders as you would want to be treated yourself.

Keeping It Real with Bidders

A fter you have written an RFP and identified a long list of potential suppliers, now you need to issue the document. Here you're triggering a more formal process, and you'll want to follow best practices, including obtaining signed NDAs (nondisclosure agreements) and making sure that you don't favor any individual bidders in your approach. You'll also want to highlight key deadlines and emphasize their importance.

Use this time to assess how bidders interact with you. How they behave in a sales process may not be a completely accurate barometer of future relations after a contract is signed, but you may learn about their overall culture and approach in ways that can and should affect your decision-making.

Setting Expectations

First, you need to set expectations. This includes the fact that you will be sharing confidential information about your organization and business, so bidders need to sign an NDA with you first. Make sure that you have one well in advance and can issue it at least a week before the RFP (request for proposal) goes out, to give the bidders a chance to review it properly before signing.

Ideally, your organization can deliver a "friendly" NDA that's not outside the norm. If your NDA is indeed fairly standard and bidders want to mark it up significantly, that's a sign that they may prove difficult in some of the more involved negotiations that are sure to come.

At this point, potential bidders will ask a lot of qualifying questions. Use your judgment about how much you want to give away at this point, but always err on the side of discretion. You do not need to reveal how many bidders are participating, what your total budget is, and any additional requirements that aren't in the RFP. Simply respond that bidders can expect a very comprehensive solicitation, that they will have ample time to ask questions in written format, and finally the kicker: that you chose them specifically after performing thorough research.

Finally, include an intent-to-bid deadline in your solicitation. Give bidders a week or so to decide, but then make them declare officially whether or not they will participate. If several bidders drop out, you may need to reassess your bearings. Try to find out why they begged off. Was the timing bad? Was the level of effort too steep relative to the potential financial reward for the vendors? Was it the wrong marketplace? It pays to know.

Even if you're a big-name customer, don't assume that just because you sent out an RFP that all or even most of the vendors will respond. Avoid these five mistakes that can discourage a vendor from participating:

1. **Acting entitled or dismissive.** You can and should be firm about what you want and the process you'll follow, but in business, as in life, politeness keeps doors open

2. **Drafting an overly long or confusing RFP.** If it takes too much effort for vendors to interpret, they'll most likely beg off

3. **Reusing canned RFPs.** Vendors will think the process is "wired" for a competitor and will avoid putting effort into a proposal

4. **Remaining vague about your authority.** Bidders want to know that your team has a clear process and authority to follow through on a real procurement

5. **Treating bidders unfairly.** Giving a bidder insufficient time to respond to a complicated RFP or RFI will lead to shallow, cookie-cutter proposals, and fewer than you expected

If only one or two drop out, that's not a big deal. Under certain circumstances, you may consider inviting a "B list" vendor, with the caveat that they'll have less time to respond.

On occasion, a bidder who has committed to participate will subsequently prove to be a no-show. Obviously, this is questionable behavior, but it happens, and so it's all the more reason to cast a wide net at this phase.

Answering Questions

At some early point in their proposal process, you need to give bidders a chance to ask written questions and obtain useful answers. First, it's only fair to them, given the amount of work you're soliciting, but also the nature of their questions can help you get to know them a little bit better. Finally, a Q&A cycle closes the gap between what you thought your RFP was communicating and how it is actually being received and interpreted by potential bidders.

Always demand questions in writing; anything else is unfair to the other bidders. Avoid awkward "bidders conferences" where they all get together on a single call or room, unless your (likely public-sector) process absolutely requires it.

Don't be surprised to experience a wide range of questions:

- Some bidders will have none, which could be a warning sign, but might also suggest that they fully understand what you're doing, or were simply too busy to focus on the RFP that early in the process.

- Some bidders will pose *a lot* of questions, perhaps under the misimpression that this shows some deep commitment to the process; however, they may be wasting their time and yours.

- Some bidders will ask questions whose answers are clearly indicated in the RFP; you don't need to include those in the final responses.

- Some bidders may send generic qualification questionnaires; you can be selective in answering them.

You'll want to turn around written answers to those questions as quickly as possible— ideally within 72 hours—so err on the side of short answers if necessary. Be polite but direct, and provide whatever supplemental data or documents that now seem necessary, if you can assemble them in time (see Figure 11.1).

What Is Your Budget?
We have received executive sponsorship for this effort and looking to spend in proportion to the value we obtain.

How Many Bidders Are Participating?
We have reached out to a good handful of plausible suppliers, after confirming through advance research that all of them could plausibly meet our needs.

On Page 2 You Say "Coupled" CRM While on Page 5 You Say "Bundled" CRM. Which One Is Correct?
Thank you for pointing out this mistake. We mean "coupled" in both cases.

Can You Share a Sample Package of Assets for Us to Use in Our Demo?
Yes, we will provide this to bidders as an annotated Zip file one week before the demo phase.

During the Demo Day Can We Show You Our Advanced AI Feature That's Not Part of Your Scenarios?
We strongly encourage you to stick to the script. If you pass to the bake-off round, we can discuss potential capabilities that weren't in our original solicitation.

FIGURE 11.1
Sample answers to typical bidder questions, mostly for you to pick up the tone: polite, authoritative, and direct.

Ideally the process works like this. You...

1. Anonymize all bidder questions, by removing any identifying information.

2. Group them into logical categories, like "Process" or "Q&A."

3. De-duplicate and combine questions as necessary.

4. Remove questions that are irrelevant, unnecessary, or simply too complicated for this phase of the process.

5. Answer each one to the depth that time allows, noting that a faster set of responses is typically better than a deeper set.

6. Share the entire resulting document to all the bidders, including the ones who did not pose any questions.

At this point, some bidders may ask for follow-up questions, based on your responses to their initial queries. Use your judgment here. If there's broad confusion among bidders, you need to address any issues directly. If a single bidder is simply niggling you, just say "no."

REAL STORY

The Media Company That Included Open Source

Open source technology platforms have long offered plausible alternatives to commercial solutions, especially for developer-intensive platforms. The challenge is that with more community-oriented open source projects, there may not be a single "vendor" to receive and respond to an RFP.

We once helped a media company that wanted to consider a community open source package alongside commercial competitors. Initially, some internal developers proposed serving as a kind of "red team" to participate on behalf of the open source option in the selection process. That obviously wasn't a good idea, as they'd be biased and didn't have the time or expertise to write proposals and build prototypes.

Instead, we found a plausible systems integration firm that specialized in that open source platform, and they responded to the RFP. To be sure, this meant accommodating a somewhat different approach and pricing model, but in the end, the customer got a strong and fair representation of what that package could do.

Lesson: Remain open to alternate business models and be creative around finding the right firm to bid on behalf of a particular technology.

Tips

- Let suppliers know in advance that they have been short-listed and to expect the RFP on a particular date.

- Confirm that you have selected them specially after conducting significant research.

- Ask bidders to sign an NDA and then later an "Intent to Respond" so that you can anticipate the volume of proposals.

- Make sure to communicate that you will not entertain any oral questions (unless you decided to do so).

- Be firm but friendly (not arrogant) in all communications.

- Do not socialize with vendor reps after issuing the RFP.

- Set aside a day of uninterrupted time to answer the questions.

- Collate, anonymize, and share questions and your answers with all the bidders.

- You do not need to answer every question, but you should answer as many as you can.

- Remain polite and open-minded in your responses.

- For more complex technologies or projects, consider inviting a second round of follow-up questions, but in any event, make sure that your schedule supports this.

- If you are considering open source options and lack a single vendor to respond, find a local integration partner who knows that platform very well.

CHAPTER 12

How to Evaluate
Proposals Critically

Reviewing proposals can serve as an illuminating first step as vendors try to address your use cases. But you'll want to give your team adequate time to read and evaluate, enabling them to pay particular attention to responses on user stories, architecture, and pricing.

Try to read "in-between" the lines to see whether the bidder is truly familiar with your business challenges. In terms of filtering to the next round, we encourage a qualitative review process over a quantitative scoring method. This phase ends with the first "downselect" meeting to narrow the field for the next round.

Critical Evaluation

Proposals can be exciting to read—*all that fantastic modern functionality!*—but this task can also become a slog for the team, so you want to do it as efficiently as possible. First, recognize that reading will take time and make sure that selection team members receive a respite from their other duties as part of your overall schedule. A useful tip is to gather the team in a conference room for a day or two to read them together.

Every member should read every proposal, but each member should focus more deeply on their areas of expertise or interest. For example, the technical team members don't necessarily need to belabor the part of the proposal about usability, nor should the business stakeholders dig deeply into security details.

Here are some specific tasks for review team members:

- Flag tasks or items from the narrative journeys that you want to examine closely during the demos.

- Identify follow-ups or clarifications from answers to the "Advanced Q&A" that you want to raise during the Q&A period or similar chalk-talk on demo day.

- Challenge assumptions and don't assume that anything you read is fully accurate until you see it with your own eyes.

When everyone has finished reading, it can be useful for the team to gather over a happy hour or some other social venue to share their impressions informally. The goal here is not to make a formal decision (that comes next), but to share information and impressions in a relaxed, social setting—often helpful lubrication for the sometimes intense discussions to follow.

CAUTION **ALIGN FINANCIAL BIDS WITH TECHNICAL PROPOSALS**

Always keep a sharp eye out for "optional" modules in any proposal and their pricing. A common tactic is to demonstrate the advanced version of a product and laud its features in a written proposal, but then price out a baseline version that offers only a scant few of the bells and whistles that drew enamored business users to the product.

In any competitive solicitation, insist that the technical proposal only discusses features and options that are priced in the core cost proposal, and that optional features and modules are clearly identified in both sections. Unfortunately, you can expect vendors to try to muddy the waters here. Keep going back to them to break it all down. This may be an iterative process, but it is well worth your effort.

The Downselect Process

An adaptive selection process will have multiple "downselect" phases where you filter to a smaller number of potential suppliers: from long list to short list, from proposals to demos, from demos to bake-off, and then ultimately selecting the finalist.

The advice here applies to all those phases, but filtering down from written proposals against your RFP is likely the first truly formal vetting exercise, so let's get into how to do it right.

First, task each individual member with documenting the good and bad about what they read (RFP) / saw (demo) / tried (bake-off). We find it most effective to just employ a simple two-by-two matrix, either a SWOT (strengths, weaknesses, opportunities, and threats) analysis or the pros and cons for both technology and vendor (see Figure 12.1).

We recommend keeping these individual assessments open-ended, where each team member can speak to their specific expertise and interests. But if you need something more structured, you can extend the rows to be more specific, e.g., separate rows for each scenario or business objective, plus architecture, TCO, and other considerations. Just don't make it too long, or your real priorities will get lost in the details.

VENDOR	CONS	PROS
ONE	• Start-up risk (schedules, quality, etc.) • Deficient on Scenario 2 • Security risk with no multifactor authentication • Weak ecosystem, especially in EMEA • Reporting is slim and dev-centric	• Technically very innovative • Did well on key Scenario 1 • Multitenancy reduces TCO • Simpler: favors configuration over customization • Strong customer support
TWO	• Weak implementation partner? • 20% higher TCO • Needed help to demo Scenario 4 • Plugin gap reduces integration utility • Proprietary repository and query language risks lock-in	• Technically robust and reliable • Strong professional services • Experience in our industry • Strong security controls • Seemed easier to use

FIGURE 12.1

Example pros and cons.

It's important to hold a formal downselect meeting, chaired by the program champion, with the PM documenting the findings. It can be useful to recruit a neutral, outside facilitator to move things along and help the team come to a good decision. (The authors often play this role.)

In advance of the meeting, everyone should *rank* the bidders and share them privately with the project manager. They can put zero for prohibitively unacceptable, a dash for any proposal they didn't read, and ties are allowed. Reassure members that their rankings are provisional, and they will have a chance to adjust them in the course of subsequent discussions.

If you are reviewing proposals or demos from, say, four vendors, very often one or two will emerge as obviously prohibitive or attractive. You can make decisions on those fairly quickly and should focus your time on areas of apparent disagreement. In the example shown in Figure 12.2, where the goal is to downselect from four to two vendors, clearly "Delta" vendor should advance to the next round.

	Aideen	Jorge	Pieter	Alysha	Tim	Stephan
ABLE	4	4	3	4	4	4
BAKER	1	1	0	2	2	3
CHARLIE	3	3	2	2	2	2
DELTA	2	2	1	1	1	1

FIGURE 12.2

Provisional rankings by a small selection team reviewing proposals from four vendors, A through D.

In the example shown in Figure 12.3, we would first give Pieter a chance to explain his prohibitive zero ranking on Baker vendor. Perhaps he sees irresolvable technical or usability problems. And perhaps those are persuasive, but on the other hand, both Aideen and Jorge ranked Baker as their top choice, so eliminating them in this round is not an easy call. Likewise, they ranked Charlie in third place, filtering that vendor out of the next round when the rest of the team ranked Charlie to move on.

	Aideen	Jorge	Pieter	Alysha	Tim	Stephan
ABLE	4	4	3	4	4	4
BAKER	1	1	0	2	2	3
CHARLIE	3	3	2	2	2	2
DELTA	2	2	1	1	1	1

FIGURE 12.3

It's helpful to highlight areas of key disagreement. For example, Pieter has designated Baker vendor as a no-go, while the rest of the team seems to be split between Baker and Charlie.

Here's where a good facilitator can get the team to the right decision by helping them align with enterprise objectives (see Figure 12.4). Selecting technology typically involves trade-offs, and savvy team leadership will always reference the original business objectives when focusing the team.

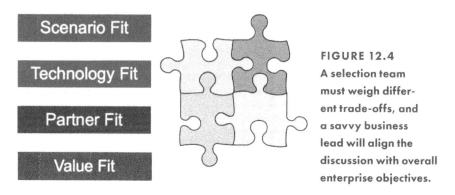

Scenario Fit

Technology Fit

Partner Fit

Value Fit

FIGURE 12.4

A selection team must weigh different trade-offs, and a savvy business lead will align the discussion with overall enterprise objectives.

In any case, the program champion leading the effort should always clarify *how* decisions will get made, understanding that there are different ways to get there (as described earlier in Chapter 3, "Get the Basic Foundations Right").

REAL STORY

When Consensus Doesn't Work

Sometimes a team can't reach consensus. This may be because participants don't trust each other or have brought baggage to the process, but more commonly they simply disagree about what they saw or the organization's relative priorities.

We once advised a financial services conglomerate selecting CRM technology. It was a major effort with a large project team, and in this case, after long discussion and analysis, the business and IT stakeholders disagreed about which vendors should advance. The IT participants were agreeable to a vote—which they would have lost—but the savvy business champion decided to employ a particular form of fiat.

We documented the key concerns and disagreements and brought the issue to an executive review board, which eventually made the decision.

To be sure, you don't typically want to punt such decisions "upstairs;" rather, you should employ such bodies for review and validation of specific recommendations from the selection team. In this case, though, it was essential for a clear decision to be made, and it created an environment where the IT team didn't feel railroaded by their colleagues, which would have boded poorly for essential future cooperation.

Lesson: When the team gets truly deadlocked, document the core disagreements and request a higher-level review board to decide on behalf of the enterprise.

When advising enterprise customers, we typically will drive toward consensus where possible. An open, comprehensive process typically lends itself to this type of decision-making, where reasonable people empathize with the needs of others and are open to changing their minds. Of course, sometimes this doesn't work.

As a result of this process, you've now downselected vendors to the demo round. Congratulations! But you still have work to do. First, catalog concerns and questions about the advancing vendors to ensure that they get addressed in the next phase. Next, explore revising your set of scenarios based on what you learned: perhaps some are too simplistic or not differentiating enough. If you've scheduled several weeks' notice for the advancing vendors, you can revise the demo scripts based on what you learned.

Tips

- Give evaluators "time off" from regular duties to read carefully, perhaps in an offsite location.

- Avoid overly complex scoring methodologies, which are typically quite unscientific.

- Adopt and modify as necessary a basic "SWOT" analysis to fit your organizational culture.

- Schedule sufficient time for a downselect meeting to consider all views.

- The most senior business stakeholder should chair the downselect meeting.

- Gather and collate written feedback in advance of the downselect meeting.

- Work to normalize and compare pricing in advance of the downselect meeting.

- Note, however, that all fees are negotiable and service costs in particular are at best a guesstimate at this stage.

- Make sure that all key stakeholders who evaluated the proposals are represented in the downselect session.

- Agree on a decision-making format in advance (e.g., consensus, voting, etc.).

- Remember that you are not making the final selection decision, but merely filtering for the next round.

- Also remember that you have only seen words and pictures, and not (a more revealing) interactive demo.

- Use the downselect meeting to prepare a recommendation or justification statement to higher governance bodies.

- Gather questions for vendors who have advanced to the next stage to make sure that they address them in their demos.

- Re-evaluate scenarios for the demo round: reduce the number and enhance the relevancy based on what you've learned.

PART V

Try Before You Buy

This is the fun part, where you start to see the technology in action, first via demos, then with hands-on testing.

Demo days—covered in Chapter 13, "Hold Demos on Your Own Terms,"—are a critical part of the filtering process, although sometimes selection teams dread them. We can understand the trepidation: demos can easily become numbing for all participants, especially when there's a disconnect between what the presenter is showing and what the buyer truly needs to see. Done right, however, demos can discriminate effectively among offerings, and just as importantly, educate all participants (vendors and buyers alike) on real business needs.

You will want to conduct competitive, hands-on testing of two finalists before selecting a supplier—what is sometimes known as a *proof-of-concept (PoC)*, *bake-off*, or *sandboxing* phase. We cover this phase in Chapter 14, "Run Competitive Proof-of-Concepts."

This kind of hands-on experience offers the best final predictor of vendor fit for you, and in the long run, it saves time and money. However, PoCs are "real" projects and require dedicated management and attention on your end.

Hold Demos on Your Own Terms

Demos serve as a kind of bridge between a narrative proposal and hands-on prototyping, taking an abstract process and making it more real. Rather than discuss what a solution could theoretically do, the bidder has to *show* your team. If planned and structured meticulously, demo sessions can be highly revealing about the technology and the vendor, as well as the true relevance of your scenarios.

Demos can and should be intense sessions, but don't stress too much about them; you're not picking the final winner, yet. Just be sure to follow the practices we lay out in the rest of this chapter.

How to Structure the Demo Sessions

The first question you'll want to answer is, "How long should the demos take"? The answer, as always, is: "How important is this technology to your enterprise?" With a structured and disciplined demo agenda, you control the pace and itinerary. At the same time, you need to be fair to vendors, giving them ample time to demo and explain, while being sure to treat each one equally.

Here are some boundaries. On simpler, SaaS-based solutions we've organized half-day demo sessions. For more complex, mission-critical tools, we've run three-day demos, although at that point you're almost conducting a PoC, which really should be the next phase. For most procurements, a single demo day for each vendor should suffice.

The key is to return to your original set of relevant user stories, spending enough time on them to allow bidders to demonstrate meaningful differences.

You can see a sample one-day itinerary in Table 13.1; let's break down each part.

- **Introductions:** Keep this brief but make sure that everyone on both teams details their role in the process.

- **Bidder overview:** This is time-boxed to keep them from blabbering on, but it can be useful contextual reinforcement to their proposal.

- **Solution intro:** Give the presenters a chance to discuss architecture, user experience fundamentals, and overall approach, as useful background to the more specific scenarios.

- **Use-case demos:** This is the meat of the day and where you'll learn more clearly the extent of their "fit."

- **Review advanced Q&A:** Ask to see key features or attributes they outlined in their proposal regarding integration, features, implementation, hosting, etc.

- **Private caucus:** Meet privately to assemble your major questions and biggest concerns about the solution, for the bidder to address.

- **Final questions:** Conduct the final questions and wrap up the day.

TABLE 13.1 SAMPLE AGENDA FOR A ONE-DAY DEMO

Time	Agenda Item	Length
9:00–9:10	Introductions	10 minutes
9:10–9:30	Brief bidder company overview	20 minutes
9:30–10:15	Introduction: architecture, approach, user experience	45 minutes
10:15–10:30	Break	15 minutes
10:30–12:00	Demonstration of user stories 1–4	90 minutes
12:00–13:00	Joint lunch break and informal chat (meal provided)	60 minutes
13:00–14:00	Continue user stories 5–6	60 minutes
14:00–15:30	Demonstrate bidder answers to "advanced Q&A"	90 minutes
15:30–16:00	Break and private selection team caucus	30 minutes
16:00–17:00	Final questions, discussion	60 minutes

The Vendor Who Wouldn't Demo the Scenarios

We were facilitating the selection of a new publishing platform for a major media company. During one of the demo days, one of the vendors ended up shell-shocking the audience by deconstructing the carefully-crafted business scenarios into a list of discrete features and functions. They listed the features on PowerPoint slides and then demoed each, one by one, outside of any business context.

When the customer asked questions outside the scope of the vendor's carefully controlled narrative, it resulted in blank stares and awkward sighs.

At that point, we had a couple of options:

1. Part ways right then and there, and not waste anyone's time. If the vendor doesn't bother parsing your use cases, would they bother responding to, say, your support tickets?

2. Put the vendor and their team in a "time-out." As childish as it sounds, isolating them in a separate room for an hour—to come up with a different approach and to re-architect the demo to focus on what you really need—can sometimes salvage a sinking day.

In this case, we went with option 1, after judging the situation irrecoverable; there was simply too much customer talent in the room to waste a day. We broke it to the vendor gently, and they had the grace to depart pleasantly. Lesson learned for all.

Lesson: Communicate clearly to bidders that your user stories best reflect your business priorities. You do not need to waste time with vendors who do not follow your process.

How to Run the Demo Sessions

For both you and the vendor, much of your success will come from proper demo prep beforehand. The week prior to the demos gather the team to review schedules and hash out all the logistics. Review the scenarios one last time so that everyone is clear about what's included—and what's not. Sensitize the team to refrain from burdening the demos with outlier questions.

Note that you'll want to ensure that the entire team participates in all of the demos. It's demoralizing for teammates and bidders alike if key members skip days or duck in and out of sessions. Also, when it comes time to evaluate and rank the bidders, itinerant team members won't be able to give complete input.

One exception to this rule is that you may want to schedule parallel, role-specific break-out sessions during the demo day, where only a subset of relevant team members participate. Examples include:

- Private negotiation sessions on contracts and pricing
- Architectural or other technical "chalk talk" sessions
- Technical vs. business Q&A
- Bidder's implementation methodology

Use the half-hour "caucus" time toward the end of the afternoon effectively, to make sure that you uncover as much as possible without having the bidder do too much follow-up. For the hour-long final Q&A, you may have time for as many as a dozen questions, but you should capture them all on a whiteboard to prioritize them. Convert any initial concerns into questions. For example, if someone found the user interfaces too difficult to use, tell the vendor straight out, then ask, "Do they always have to work that way, or could they be simplified?"

For the final question of the day, we always like to ask, "What's something important that we [the customer] need to know about you or your solution that we haven't already asked?" That gives the bidder a chance to fill you in on something potentially important before they depart.

At the end of each demo day, try to have the team stay for an extra half-hour for a group "wash-up" on what they saw. The facilitator can capture and organize initial pros and cons while still fresh in minds, with the understanding that this does not yet represent a final assessment.

You may uncover some quirks in your scenarios that you didn't expect. Perhaps you didn't explain something well, or some tasks turn out to be much more important than others. Use that learning to improve the scripts for the PoC phase. But resist the temptation to change the process too much during the demo phase; remember the vendors have prepped for what's in your RFP, and after having had a chance to ask questions, they should be well prepared to deliver on what you requested. Don't throw a spanner in the works at this point.

At Real Story Group, we only work on behalf of technology buyers and don't advise vendors, but after sitting in on hundreds of technology vendor demos, we'll break with tradition and offer eight tips to vendor demo teams:

1. **Show up early.** Among other things, you'll want to figure out the connectivity situation in advance.

2. **Invest in decent tools.** You want to have a solid demo environment since the competitor's sales engineer who came yesterday ran through her use cases flawlessly in a top-flight cloud environment that didn't hiccup on her.

3. **Be prepared for this particular customer.** You'll see some very specific scripts and questions. If you don't respect that effort, you can lose something more important than the deal: *your reputation.*

4. **Don't ignore bugs.** As every vendor will confess, bugs are part of demos, especially when the customer creates a custom script. Acknowledge the bug, take a stab at explaining it, and try to fix it at the break.

5. **Test your demo that day.** Your best prevention against catastrophic failure is to test your environment and any remote services against the use cases *just before* your demo begins (remember, you came early).

6. **Don't argue amongst yourselves.** Before the demo, sort out the functional, financial, or business division of labor among the team, or it will surely come out in the demo.

7. **Remember that show beats tell.** Show *how* your technology works, rather than just talk to it. People will remember screens—and what they thought when they saw them—long after they've forgotten spoken words.

8. **Pay attention to what the customer actually requested.** A strong agenda will allow extra time for a vendor to be creative, but if it comes at the expense of demonstrating something essential, it can backfire.

After the final demo, you'll want to schedule a downselect meeting as soon as possible, while impressions are still fresh. During that meeting, be sure to capture all the changes you want to make to the use cases prior to the PoC, so that when you get hands-on, you're working with the best approximation of what you're looking for.

Demo Pitfalls to Avoid

So now that you have a plan, schedule, and team buy-in, let's review four demo-day pitfalls to avoid.

- **Don't drown out questions, but watch for edge cases.**

  During the demos, individuals on your team will likely start asking a lot of questions. Of course, there are no bad questions, but there *is* bad timing. Keep a whiteboard "parking lot" for things that feel obscure, or only relate to one person's job, or have to do with a minor exception rather than a major business objective. Remember that you have at least an hour later in the day to come back to them.

  Above all, you want to keep the flow of the demos going: you asked for important services and the vendor prepped them, so give bidders a chance to complete them.

- **Keep on keeping it real.**

  If you follow the structure we lay out, your demo days will emphasize *doing* over *talking.* An interactive experience becomes much more useful than PowerPoint slides. When vendors start to get abstract, insist on the former and closely time-box the latter. An operative question, especially for the Q&A phase, is "Can you actually demonstrate what you mean by that?"

- **Pay attention to scope.**

  Oftentimes, a bidder will want to show you some nifty capability that lies outside the scope of your use cases. You might respond enthusiastically and the sales team will depart thinking they won a great coup. But then later—always later—calmer heads will prevail and someone will remind their fellow selection team members, "Hey, they never showed us X, or Y, or Z!" Suspicions arise, and the vendor's not around to allay them. Best to stick to your script.

- **Ask the hard questions.**

  Amid the bonhomie of a productive demo, both you and the vendor might become tempted to "park" weak or uncomfortable topics, including performance, security, usability, and pricing, among others. Remember that you will want to decide who moves on to the next round shortly after the final vendor demo, while all the screens and interactions remain fresh in your mind. So ask the hard questions and give candid feedback about weaknesses; it respects everyone's time and gets you to the right fit faster.

Tips

- Make sure that the entire selection team can attend all demos; it's only fair.

- Hold a demo prep meeting with the team to educate and set expectations.

- Give yourself and the vendor enough demo time, typically a full day.

- Consider "double-tracking" part of the day to have separate technical and business sessions for larger or more complex projects.

- Make sure that the vendor is only demoing shipping products (not future) and only the modules they priced, unless explicitly noted otherwise.

- Allow for a private caucus session preceding a final Q&A segment.

- Make sure that everyone on your team is using the same evaluation form.

- Remember that a strong chair needs to keep things moving along.

- Keep a separate list of unanswered questions and give bidders a deadline for written responses.

- Avoid vendor sleights of hand where they show you something off-script to distract your attention from a shortcoming.

- After the demo, hold a quick recap meeting among your team.

- Begin clarifications and negotiations with vendor account reps in a separate meeting that same day.

- Remember that the goal is not to identify an ideal vendor—which doesn't exist —but the best "fit" for the subsequent hands-on bake-off.

- Avoid the temptation to downselect to a single vendor; try to set up a competitive PoC to make the best decision.

- On the other hand, do not invite a bidder to the PoC phase if you are certain you would never select them.

Run Competitive Proof-of-Concepts

In the context of a technology selection project, a "bake-off" is really a competitive proof-of-concept where the two vendor finalists are asked to mimic a real implementation sprint, and then show you how to get hands-on with at least some parts of their proposed solution. Sometimes called *sandboxing* or *PoC*, at some level, it's the most important part of the selection process because it simulates working with both the solution and potentially the implementation team.

In this bake-off, you'll use your ingredients (content and data), your bakers (participating employees), and your kitchen (your real environments)—although as you'll see later, sometimes you have to use the vendor's kitchen.

Like all good things, a useful bake-off takes time and attention, since the mechanics can get tricky. But the payoff is worth it.

This chapter will enumerate best practices for justifying and then conducting a sandboxed competition, addressing topics such as: who funds, how long, who participates, and how to make a good final decision.

The Case for a Bake-Off

You will sometimes hear consultants, analysts, and vendors make the argument that bake-offs are too time- and resource-intensive—and ultimately they are a waste of time. Well, they are partly right. Bake-offs *can* be a waste of time for the vendors that don't get selected or the consultants and analysts that get paid only when a final choice has been made by their client.

However, bake-offs are almost never a waste of time for the enterprise that is actually buying the technology:

- You will have time and information to negotiate a better-fitting deal.

- You will avoid the potentially heavy cost of a bad choice.

- You should get to a pilot implementation faster.

The business case for a PoC offers more than just risk reduction. By testing vendors before you select them, you can obtain several other benefits:

- By comparing solutions apples-to-apples in an empirical way, you can save time by readily justifying the decision to review boards, using concrete criteria.

- By engaging end-users in the selection process in a way that feels relevant and useful to them, via hands-on testing, it bodes well for their support during tough implementation times.

- Testing your own requirements against reality enables you to reprioritize your objectives midstream, before you're locked into a particular supplier.

- This sort of prototyping allows you to jump-start your initial implementation and reduce the time from contract to value.

- By learning (most of) the shortcomings of the winning vendor, you can plan around them.

- You get a better sense for realistic implementation costs before you select a solution, and you also gain some valuable time and space to negotiate the best deal.

Yes, there's still a cost to running a bake-off, but in the end, what's the cost of a failed implementation?

CAUTION **RESIST THE TEMPTATION TO TAKE SHORT-CUTS**

Sometimes, enterprise leaders will challenge the idea of doing competitive bake-offs. Why not save time and money and just test the single highest-ranking vendor coming out of the demo?

There are several reasons *not* to do this:

- With nothing to compare against, you can never ascertain if that vendor is truly the best fit.

- You learn less about yourself and your true needs.

- You lose negotiation leverage, as the vendor inevitably discovers that it's not a competitive situation.

- The overall frame of reference changes subtly against you, as the effort becomes more about how you could make it work, rather than is this the right partner.

Finally, the putative leader out of the demos doesn't always win in the end. Check out this real story.

REAL STORY

We helped a large hospital select a new digital asset management system for their marketing collateral. After the vendor demo phase, the selection team identified two finalists, but Vendor A emerged as the clear leader at that point.

It was tempting to just abandon the bake-off plan and simply start the implementation with Vendor A. However, in the interest of full due diligence, the hospital went ahead with a two-week bake-off, their marketing and IT teams working side-by-side with each vendor's implementation team.

At the end of the bake-off, the team learned the following information:

- While Vendor A's user experience had dazzled them during the demos, for the hospital's most common, workaday use case, Vendor B's workflow and interface proved simpler to use for the marketing team.

- For the hospital's most important content type (high-res photos), Vendor B was able to demonstrate much faster ingestion times.

- Regarding all-important mobile access to the systems, certain key functionality was missing with Vendor A. (This never came up in the demos.)

- When the marketing team reached out to each of the vendor's help desks, Vendor A's help desk never responded, while Vendor B's help desk responded immediately.

As you can imagine, Vendor B won the deal, and the hospital went on to a successful implementation.

Final lesson: Try before you buy!

How to Run a Bake-Off

A PoC week is similar to a demo week inasmuch as it requires a lot of preparation and can be very time-intensive (but usually productive!) for the selection team. As with the demos, you'll want to make sure that the full team gets briefed in advance and has their calendars (mostly) cleared to participate.

Likewise, make sure that the vendor preps in advance. They may need to modify their demo implementations based on changes you made to the use cases after that first round. Or they may need to polish up some of the user experience to prep for your hands-on work. And they will need to prepare both business and IT training for your team.

Here's a demo schedule for a one-week PoC (see Figure 14.1).

ACME TEAMS: IT Team		Business Team	Management Team
Monday, July 27–need to plan with team			
Morning		Business User training	Business User training
Afternoon		Business User training	Business User training
End of Day		Status meeting and feedback	Status meeting and feedback
Tuesday, July 28–need to plan with team			
Morning	Tech Chalk Talk	Ongoing testing	
Afternoon	Dev Training	Ongoing testing	
End of Day	Status meeting and feedback	Status meeting and feedback	Status meeting and feedback
Wednesday, July 29			
Morning	Time Off (Vendor Dev Sprint to Make Adjustments)		
Afternoon	Time Off (Vendor Dev Sprint to Make Adjustments)		Review final bid jointly w/ vendor
End of Day: 3–4	Status meeting and feedback	Status meeting and feedback	Status meeting and feedback
Thursday, July 30			
Morning	Ongoing testing	Ongoing testing	
Afternoon	Ongoing testing	Ongoing testing	
End of Day: 3–4	Status meeting and feedback	Status meeting and feedback	Status meeting and feedback
Friday, July 31–need to plan with team			
Morning	Wrap-up with final Q&A and sample migration results; then Vendor departs		
Afternoon	Brief Internal Team Caucus		

KEY:
Full ACME Team
IT Team: Primarily Devs and Architects
Business Team: Editorial and Managers
Management Team: Contracts
Vendor Team

FIGURE 14.1

Sample one-week schedule for PoC with three different customer teams interacting with the vendor. See the appendix, "Resources and Examples," for a link to a soft copy.

Remember the goal of the PoC is to perform hands-on assessments, so the first thing to consider is the primacy of training—for both business and IT team members. You will likely need at least a full day for each, possibly two. Note that this doesn't have to be comprehensive training in the solution—just enough to be able to impersonate specific personas and run the use cases by yourself.

For the rest of the week, you'll want to run essentially a series of sprints, where the vendor and perhaps your team members are modifying the environment and answering your questions as you get more comfortable.

This is also a good time to have more specialized sessions, such as:

- Architecture, security, and other technical chalk talks
- Financial and contract negotiations
- Development operations ("devops") reviews and tests
- Trial data migrations from any incumbent systems

If you anticipate a more developer-heavy, platform-type environment where the vendor or your team may be performing substantial customizations as part of the PoC, then consider giving the vendor a day off to make interim fixes on their own. It also gives them a chance to experiment a bit with the test environment you're using while you're not online. This also gives your team a break to get other work done!

Bake-Off FAQs

Typically, bake-offs can engender a lot of questions. Remember, first, that there are no hard rules, but here are some provisional answers to questions we frequently field.

Should we hold the bake-offs in parallel or serial?

Serial, for sure. They are a lot of work and require a commitment of time on behalf of your team and some logistical effort to host the bidder team. Schedule a week's break in-between the bake-offs to allow your colleagues to get their "real" work done.

Do we need to pay for the PoC?

In all likelihood, yes; this is also good motivation for vendors to participate. Sometimes, a vendor's sales' or services' arm can participate gratis in a PoC as a cost of sale. Services firms typically require some sort of fee. But you should never pay list price. Instead, ask in your RFP for the bidders to propose a fee for their participation, at a discounted rate, and, of course, you can negotiate that. Often, bidders will dispense with some or all of the cost if you end up selecting them, so you only pay the vendor who didn't make it, similar to "kill fees" in publishing.

What if we want to test and ultimately deploy the solution on-premise?

Most of the time, vendors will set up PoC instances in a cloud that everyone can access; it's simpler that way. If you are considering an on-premise deployment, it still might make sense to test it in the cloud. If you want to try out the actual installation, though, we'd recommend doing so, with the vendor's help, *before* the bake-off, so that all the potential systems' snags get addressed prior to digging into the business scenarios.

How do we address complicated technical topics like integration, security, and performance?

Ask as many questions as possible and review systems and code together, but once again, doing is better than seeing. For integration, you may be able to simulate or build some simple integration cases into the PoC scenarios. In any event, you'll need to make sure that your own systems are ready to go, including port numbers and access rights. You can also run performance and security tests, but ideally you should pick a time when businesspeople are not accessing the system. Where performance is critical, we've advised customers to select a vendor provisionally, based on a functional fit, and then bring the vendor back for another week of intense technical due diligence.

How do we distinguish technical fit from implementer compatibility?

At some level, you can't: a good fitting solution will likely prove easier to implement, and an exceptionally copasetic implementation team will cover for many technical flaws. At the end of the day, you want to assess both, but just remember that while integrators and consultancies come and go, hopefully you'll keep the technology for a long time. So focus first on solution and vendor fit, including the broader ecosystem, and then turn to implementer compatibility.

After the second vendor completes the PoC, you should have a full team meeting to rank the finalists and review pros and cons against your business objectives, just like you did for the RFP and demo rounds. For advice on how to make the final selection, check out Part VI, "Make the Right Choice."

Tips

- PoCs require careful planning and project management.

- Identify and flesh out key scenarios for the vendor to implement.

- Set your team's expectations in a planning meeting about how "polished" the vendor's work is likely to be.

- You may need to reimburse bidders for their time, but at a cut rate—negotiate here.

- The ideal PoC is one to two weeks long, but may be extended for mission-critical or performance-intensive applications, or shortened for simpler technologies.

- Schedule daily "check-ins" with the vendor.

- Schedule early PoC trainings with your full team; you want to be hands-on.

- Use this time to negotiate pricing and terms while still in a competitive environment.

- If there's something you don't like about a vendor or technology, it's likely to only get worse over time, so address it explicitly.

PART VI

Make the Right Choice

You've completed the filtering process, and now you have some final decisions to make. While you should begin pricing and contract negotiations early in the process, now you need to see those discussions through to a final deal. Chapter 15, "Negotiate Like a Pro," gives you some specific advice about how to obtain the best value and the best terms.

You also need to organize the final selection between the two finalists after getting very familiar with their offerings during the bake-off. Chapter 16, "Make the Right Final Selection," will help you overcome some potential hitches here.

Finally, you may find yourself organizing a separate selection process for a services firm—an interactive agency, systems integrator, or some other consultancy—to help with the implementation or provide other support for your digital initiatives. Here again, you'll want to follow an iterative, experience-rich process, but with a few twists. Chapter 17, "Adapt This Process for Selecting Services Firms," explains how to adapt the process you used for technology vendors to find the best-fitting services partner.

CHAPTER 15

Negotiate Like a Pro

Most organizations struggle to fathom vendor price quotes, and with good reason, since suppliers often apply arcane, confusing fee models. Beware that costs can run higher than you originally expected, but following some best practices can prepare you for negotiating a fair price from a position of strength.

Similarly, contract negotiations can become highly byzantine, but are no less important. We won't offer legal advice here, but will suggest some key areas and terms to which you should pay special attention.

When to Start Negotiations

First, remember that list pricing is always negotiable, and in larger deals—those over six figures—discounts may prove to be substantial. Smaller deals and those that are less technology-heavy and more services-related may see less room for flexibility.

Like auto dealers, technology sales people will try to create a friendly relationship in an attempt to head off potentially difficult conversations. Remain businesslike throughout, and that means beginning to negotiate pricing as early in the process as possible, and then continuing to move the chains throughout the selection process.

The vendor will resist this on two grounds:

- They want to avoid expending effort until they see they are close to winning the project.

- They want to defer negotiations until after you've selected them, reducing your leverage markedly.

Make it clear throughout the vetting process that price is a key factor in your decision at each stage of the downselection process. This way, you can ask bidders to sharpen their pencils at each phase, from RFP to demos, from demos to PoC, and again during the final bake-off.

Vendors in the same marketplace can exhibit very different pricing models. Indeed, pricing can vary by a combination of the following:

- Seats
- Servers or CPU-equivalents
- Instances (including virtual containers)
- Storage
- Content volumes
- Usage
- Addressable URLs

- Add-on modules
- Service level agreement (SLA) tiers
- Bundled services hours
- And more...

So make sure that one of your team members is a spreadsheet wizard who can work to "normalize" pricing across all the proposals and develop a total cost of ownership (TCO) across a three- to five-year period. This allows you to perform an apples-to-apples comparison among bidders, but also uncover where there's extra fat in a vendor's proposal.

> **CAUTION** DON'T ASSUME THAT THE VENDOR REALLY BELIEVES YOU'RE SPECIAL
>
> Don't assume that because you're a big-name firm you represent such a good catch that vendors will accommodate you in negotiations without you having to work too hard.
>
> In fact, you may encounter the opposite: a salesperson under pressure from their manager to extract a certain fee level from you, based on your size. Vendors typically have all the top-tier customers they need; their focus is solely on meeting sales targets.
>
> You should recognize that when dealing with larger vendors, you are up against world-class sales negotiators. Negotiate early when you still have leverage and then iterate often.

Align Price and Value

Sometimes, cost negotiations are about line-item charges, but most technology vendors are smarter than that, and will try to wring extra value through arcane pricing models and a cornucopia of add-on modules.

You cannot ask too few questions here. Take the time before and after any demo to get complete clarity on financial proposals and their alignment with the technology proffered. Ensure that the technical proposal only includes features and options that are priced in the core cost proposal—and vice-versa—and that optional features and modules get clearly identified.

A common tactic in enterprise software is to demonstrate the advanced version of a platform and laud its features in a written proposal, but then price out a baseline version that offers only a scant few of the bells and whistles that enamored you during the demos. This is called *sandbagging* and is totally unethical, but alas, still endemic in the technology world.

Getting clarity and alignment can become yet another iterative process, but still well worth your effort. Be sure that all of the modules, editions, and components you need are accounted for in the final pricing bundle; get it in writing that anything found missing will be provided free of charge.

The overall goal here is to align your costs with actual business value obtained, by paying a fair price for the things you need most, and either not including or paying very little for extras that won't drive ample, near-term business value. *Near-term* is a key concept here, since the vendor is typically incented to load you up with as much functionality as possible in the initial contract, while you want to defer spending on extras until such time that they deliver business value.

CAUTION UNDERSTAND HUNTERS VERSUS FARMERS

There's a structural reason for vendors trying to front-load contracts with modules you may not need until down the road.

First-time deals typically get landed by a new business manager (a.k.a., "hunter"), who then goes away after handing you off to a key account manager (a "farmer") once a contract gets signed. The hunter typically only wants to sell licenses—as much as possible in a given quarter—and does not usually participate in a long-term relationship. He wants to load up as much as he can in an initial "kill" before seeking new prey.

The farmer, by contrast, wants to keep you happy, but also looks for genuine opportunities to sell you more services and tools as they understand your needs better. It's almost always a good idea to defer as much of your spending as possible until a farmer can prove to you empirically that you will benefit adequately from it.

The hunter has many techniques to get you to overbuy up-front, such as enticing bulk discounts. Stay disciplined and only buy what you need in the near term, but pocket those offers and then bring them up down the road when negotiating any add-ons.

Contracts and Other Agreement Negotiations

In the RFP/RFD, you asked the bidders to append their standard agreement language. Have your legal/procurement team comb through the details carefully. Like the vendors, your specialists may want to defer this diligence on efficiency grounds until a single finalist is accepted. See if you can get them to bend a bit so that negotiating terms becomes part of the selection process, where you have more leverage.

We are not barristers and won't give you legal advice, but in our experience, some hidden "gotchas" can emerge in predictable places:

- **Indemnification:** You may be financially responsible if the vendor subsumes some code or modules for which they don't have full rights.

- **Use of your name and logo:** If you are agreeable to that, then make sure that you get something really valuable in return.

- **Concurrent versus named seat licenses:** Concurrent is more attractive if you have a lot of people who will use the system sparingly.

- **Code escrow:** It's somewhat overrated, since it's not an ideal amelioration if the vendor goes bust—but it's better than nothing.

- **Competitor exclusions:** You may want either to prevent the vendor from working with a competitor, or at least prevent them from sharing your innovations with other customers in your marketplace; expect to pay extra for this.

The advent of cloud-based delivery models brings particularly thorny issues that should be addressed in any agreement:

- Uptime guarantees, with penalties for excessive downtime

- Data residency, especially for non-U.S. organizations or divisions

- Digital data shredding (not just "deletion") and conversely, long-term retention for data that you *do* need to keep

- Vendor data access and usage rights (including "aggregate" metrics)

- Security controls, including vendor employee access to your environment

- Use-it-or-lose it clauses for producers, advisors, or any support hours that come with your subscription (be sure to carry over those hours)

Tips

- Price and contract negotiations are an iterative process that you should start as early as possible.

- Normalize pricing quotes from competing suppliers over a five-year period, using your own template.

- Radically different price points from competing suppliers could reflect a very different understanding of your environment or different levels of service; probe and ask questions.

- Do not forget the costs of associated professional services.

- Do not overpay for yearly maintenance and support (20% is average) and make sure that it covers upgrades.

- Make the vendor identify optional modules that are not included in their bid.

- You can frequently negotiate 20–50% discounts on licensing, but bidders will prove to be more stubborn on services and hosting rates.

- Never buy licenses for a potential future need, no matter how good a deal is proffered; instead, drag the buying process out over time: buy only what you need, when you need it, and in the order that you need it.

- When working with cloud suppliers, review SLAs, data ownership, data security, and data disposition clauses very carefully.

- Look for indemnification clauses in contracts, especially where a vendor is embedding open source or third-party modules that may risk an intellectual property claim later.

CHAPTER 16

Make the Right Final Selection

B ased on what transpired in the competitive PoC phase, as well as cost-value considerations, your next step is to decide on the ultimate solution. In our experience—after hands-on exposure to the technology, vendor, and potentially implementation team—a clear winner typically emerges. You just want to ensure that you've taken a full measure of the choices before signing any contract.

Taking the Full View

At this stage, you want to ensure that you're taking a holistic view of what life would be like with this particular solution. As you evaluate the two offerings, put together all the pieces:

- Reference checks
- Vendor/partner fit
- Ecosystem
- Technology/solution fit
- Pricing and terms

Let's address each one in turn.

You can conduct reference checks at any time in the process, but we recommend doing so during the bake-off between two finalists. (See the appendix, "Resources and Examples," for a link to a list of questions to consider asking.) If one of the customers is local, try to do an in-person site visit instead. Reference calls and visits are particularly helpful in uncovering "intangibles" about the system and vendor: attributes like support quality and corporate culture that might not reveal themselves fully during a bake-off.

In terms of the ecosystem, in addition to potentially vetting any channel implementation partners (more about that in Chapter 17, "Adapt This Process for Selecting Services Firms"), you'll want to dip into the vendor's broader ecosystem (see Figure 16.1). Make sure to participate in some customer/developer forums—either vendor-hosted extranets or open boards. Or better yet, attend in-person user group meetings.

These will reveal the day-to-day concerns and opportunities among your potential future peers. In particular, watch out for these questions:

- How fast do support questions get answered?
- How vibrant are the discussions?
- How much do customers and integrators share ideas, code, or solution sets?

- How frequently (and where) do customers convene in person?

- How broad is the mix of potential channel partners (from indie developers to large integrators and everything in-between)?

- How much do specialists at the vendor itself participate in solving problems?

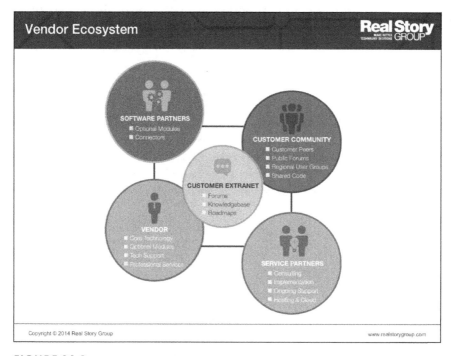

FIGURE 16.1

The strength of the vendor's ecosystem could have as much impact on your success as its technical fit.

When it comes to pricing and terms, you should have already normalized the bids and gone through at least two rounds of negotiations—not quite "best and final," but ideally pretty close. When you've settled on a finalist, you can conduct final price negotiations, although at this point, you may have less leverage.

For technology that's important to your organization, you don't want to decide based on lowest cost, but highest value, as long as you can stay within any preset budget limitations. Don't worry if you can't accurately quantify the "benefit" side of this ratio. Typically, an open discussion among the team can yield a good sense for the relative upsides of the two finalists to compare against their long-term TCO.

In terms of functional and vendor fit, at the end of a solid bake-off, most enterprises have a good sense of this. Yet if you still believe too many unknowns remain to make a decision, you can and should take additional time and devise additional tests as needed to get comfortable with any supplier or solution before settling on them. You can't squeeze out *all* the unknowns, but you'll want to make sure that you address the major ones, such as security, scalability, usability, and essential integration facilities.

REAL STORY

The Media Firm That Kept Probing

We worked with a national media conglomerate that produced several cable television networks, magazines, and boutique digital properties. They were selecting a new web content and experience management (WCM) solution that obviously would become a core platform for their business.

After going through a bake-off, one of the two finalists emerged as a clear leader in terms of functional fit and long-term value. But the customer's IT team still had some questions around performance and scalability. So they invited the vendor back for a week of additional stress testing to address those concerns.

Then the customer wanted to understand how the vendor's offering would fit with some of their aggressive future plans around micro-services architectures. A day-long brainstorming session with the vendor's lead product manager gave them enough comfort level to proceed.

Note that in both post-PoC engagements, the customer modestly compensated the vendor for their time and structured the sessions as joint learning opportunities, rather than straight-up tests, which made it more interesting and productive for the bidder as well. But make no mistake: the vendor was indeed getting tested, and fortunately, in this case they passed.

Lesson: For a mission-critical system, a prudent customer will take the time to sweat the important details.

Making the Decision

Even if there is tacit agreement on the team on the PoC winner, you need to hold one last meeting to formally capture the decision, following the decision-making process described in Chapter 3, "Get the Basic Foundations Right." Use this session to document the rationale for your choice and prepare for the next steps.

But what if you still cannot agree on a winning vendor? A savvy leader will refer back to the original business objectives and push the team to map competing bidders against anticipated outcomes, rather than more tactical concerns.

If the team still can't make a decision, then you likely have an institutional disconnect that new technology will not solve and perhaps will even aggravate. The selection team chair may become tempted to apply a decision here by fiat, but we'd encourage you to reconsider: if after vigorous empirical testing and analysis the team remains split, then you should reassess your bearings. Perhaps you are not considering the right marketplace, or you are asking too much of one solution, or the organization simply isn't ready for new technology. Or perhaps you need to address some deep-seated internal conflicts. Much like the arrival of children never solves marital woes, implementing software never mends internal business rifts.

Yet we are happy to report that in the vast majority of cases, if you follow the methods in this book, a clear winner will emerge. Now you'll want to set yourself up for success going forward.

Planning for Success

As you finalize the contract terms with the finalist, now comes the time to shift from vetting to implementation.

As a first step, you'll need to identify the inevitable shortcomings of the winning system. Perhaps the interface remains a bit cluttered. Or there are small hitches with the way it integrates with your identity management environment. Get prepared to communicate this to other colleagues to avoid unpleasant surprises, but also devise mitigation plans so that you can reduce the impact of those drawbacks.

Also, you will almost certainly need to plan for internal process and information changes. Perhaps the new system will support a more streamlined workflow, but this will still necessitate staff cooperation and understanding. Or the new platform will enable personalized customer experiences, but this will require new content variants; someone needs to compose that material. The longer you put off business change, the more you will postpone obtaining value from your new technology.

You have avoided a "waterfall" process during your selection and should continue to do so when planning the implementation. Especially for larger or more mission-critical implementations, identify a good pilot or series of pilots rather than a "big bang" implementation. Resist the temptation to make your first pilot something too simple, or you won't learn enough. But also avoid the most complicated or high-profile use-case at first, since your first go-round with the new technology will often prove less than optimal.

Finally, celebrate your decision. Hold a party! You undertook a team effort, and ideally that same team can transition from joint vetting to collaborative implementation.

Tips

- Conduct and review reference checks.

- Don't underestimate "vendor intangibles" in considering overall fit.

- Ask more questions and continue testing beyond the PoC if significant questions or concerns remain outstanding.

- Revisit implementation strategy, plans, and pricing.

- Incorporate the latest results from ongoing financial and contract negotiations.

- Hold off on licensing the complete solution until you finish the next (pilot) phase.

- Make a list of problems and shortcomings with the winning system so that you can work on mitigation plans.

CHAPTER 17

Adapt This Process for Selecting Services Firms

ervices firms often prove essential to successful implementations and enhancements, especially in the early phases of your program, where even the most well-resourced internal team may lack specific tool or domain expertise. Indeed, for larger technology projects, the majority of the overall expense typically falls here.

So budget accordingly but also choose carefully.

Even for software-as-a-service (SaaS-based) deployments—where nominally there may not be very many buttons and levers to adjust— you'll still have decisions to make about where, when, what, and how you implement the system. So you may want to avail yourself of outside expertise (even beyond the vendor) in making and then executing on those decisions.

What Sort of Help Do You Need?

Recall from our discussion in Chapter 7, "Find More Than the Usual Suspects," that you can choose from among a variety of different types of services outfits:

- Consultancies
- Agencies
- Integrators
- Vendor PSO

Over the life span of your technology investment, you may rely on all of these categories of support (see Figure 17.1). Just make sure to map the right supplier to the right phase of your product. For example:

- Consultants may help you with up-front, "soft skill" work, like process and information analysis.
- The vendor's PSO (professional services organization) will have the greatest impact during an initial implementation.
- A digital agency or systems integrator can provide continuity over multiple years.

Regardless of type, services firms will fall into different sizes and shapes as well. Here's a short summary of four categories in Table 17.1, with pros and cons.

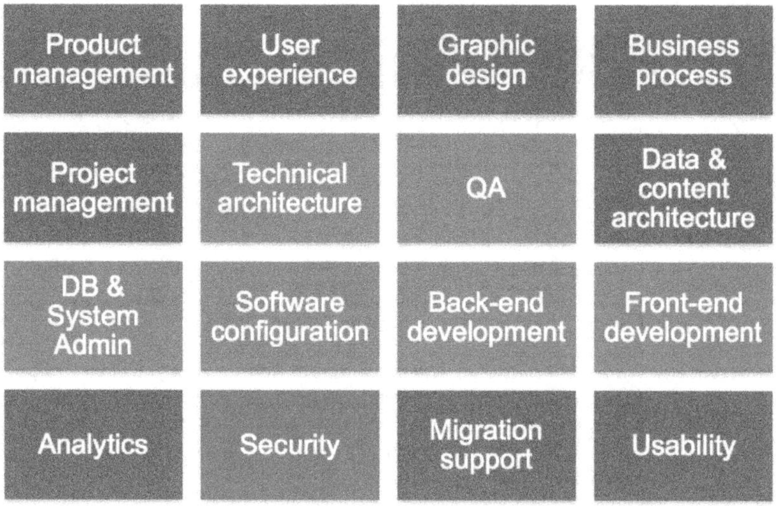

FIGURE 17.1

Depending on the scope of the technology, you may need external help in a variety of different areas. The purple boxes represent traditional integrator skills, while the green may be better delivered by agency-type firms. Of course, there are overlaps, and you might find a single firm with multiple teams that can deliver on all these services.

Note that at different times in the lifecycle of any technology, you may need different types of help from different sizes of firms. In an ideal situation, you will have a roster of diverse, go-to sources of support.

But in every case, you should vet these suppliers, just as you vetted the technology vendors. Perform this diligence in proportion to your level of spend and the criticality of the work. For a single indie developer, you can interview the person and then test them out for a day to a week. For a global design agency or consultancy, you'll want to undertake a full-blown, competitive selection process. So that's what we'll address next.

TABLE 17.1 DIFFERENT TYPES OF SERVICES FIRMS

Size and Shape	Pros	Cons	Use to...
Sole Practitioner	Can prove lower cost, offer specialized or contingent expertise on a tool or particular topic	By definition, can't scale either in terms of output or breadth of expertise	Augment your staff on a small project or provide highly specialized expertise on a contingent basis
Boutique Firm	Highly specialized expertise and knowledge	"One-trick pony" regarding a tool or area of expertise	Lead small or highly specialized projects
Regional or National	Deeper bench can handle larger projects and multiple engagements, potentially across regions	Tends to want to work on bigger projects, and may offer less continuity in terms of staff	Help you deploy larger implementations, or undertake multiyear engagements
Global	Can address the most complex and multinational projects, potentially at lower cost with successful offshoring	Size and complexity of firm can make them difficult to work with	Outsource significant chunks of your effort

How to Adapt Your Process

When selecting a services firm, you should follow the same key tenets in many respects as when choosing technology: iterative, adaptive, team-based, and above all, empirical.

As you did with the technology, assemble an interdisciplinary selection team, chaired by a business leader. Even if the work to be performed is largely nontechnical, you'll still want to involve some IT folk so they can better understand how the overall process will mesh. Likewise, if you are selecting a technology-oriented integrator, you should also involve business (and not just IT) stakeholders, who will have to work closely with this firm in any case.

Then set up a test-based process. This will differ a bit since testable user stories often don't make sense in this context. But still you want to simulate the work that the services firm will do, so invite them to do more than just describe their methodology; rather, have them lead you through some mock sprints with them, both in the demo round and then (in a more detailed way) the bake-off.

Mock sprints for a creative agency might include:

- Joint persona development exercise
- Sample customer/employee user journey development
- Provisional high-level project plan
- Mock creative brief brainstorm
- And so on...

Mock sprints for an integrator might include:

- Mini joint application design (JAD) session for some discreet piece of functionality
- Pair programming an extension with your developers
- Creation of a trial systems architecture
- And so on...

And once again, be sure to iterate and adapt your process as necessary. In a written proposal perhaps, ask them to mock up a sample persona, and then during the demo day, you can spend two hours together refining it or creating a new one Finally, in the bake-off, you can switch gears and flesh out some user journeys for that persona. The overall goal is identical to the software selection process: get beyond talking and transition to *doing* so that you can see for yourself what it would *really* be like to work with that services firm.

CAUTION BEWARE BELLS AND WHISTLES

Just like vendors will show you cool features to try to dazzle you, so too will services firms try to entice you to lean their way before you even have a chance to put them to the test.

- For initial meetings, creative agencies may create clever mock-ups and come bearing interesting gifts and enticing dinner invitations. That all seems fun and cool, but typically has little bearing on their fitness for you.

- Systems integrators will tout past clients and the difficult problems they solved, but may downplay the cost and customer level of effort required to get there.

Give yourself the time and space to probe, ask questions, check references, and above all simulate real project activities with the team proposed to work with you.

The way that you evaluate a services firm will also differ a bit from a software provider. Here's a short list of considerations:

- **Team dynamics:** How closely does their team cooperate with each other and with you?

- **Process and methodology:** On paper, many services firms have similar methodologies, but you'll notice key differences if you actually try them out.

- **Communications skills:** These are essential for success!

- **Understanding of your needs:** How much do they grasp the implications of your culture, size, and industry segment?

- **Mastery of relevant technology:** This is especially important for integrators, but sometimes important for nontechnical consulting work as well.

In terms of contracts and pricing, all the advice we offered earlier in this section for technology providers also applies here, with a couple key addenda related to the fact that you are now purchasing individuals' time and knowledge.

So, for contracts, make sure that you insert "key personnel" clauses. Ideally, these will identify individual specialists that you met and liked during the bake-off. Bidders may push back and say "or equivalent person." There's room to negotiate here; if it's a big project and the firm is reluctant to commit key staff in writing, that's a real red flag.

In terms of pricing, you'll need to isolate an overall number (at least a well-documented estimate) on the engagement rather than leave it open-ended or purely time-and-materials pricing. But pay even closer attention to hourly rate structures and utilization on the project. One bidder may propose lower-priced people, but then place a lot of them on your project. Conversely, a bidder may want to make you pay for senior people who don't ever do much; never pay for an account rep's time, for example.

Tie payments to deliverables and not the level of effort. Make sure that the overall budget aligns costs with value. That is, that the services firm is not overstaffing against side projects of smaller business impact, and that its highest-cost individuals are performing truly high-value work for you.

Tips

- Services firms can be critical to your success, so you vet them with the same care that you vetted the core technology.

- Do not limit your choices to a single channel partner that the technology vendor may have identified during the selection process, but rather avail yourself of a full set of choices, particularly if it's a larger project.

- Consider the diversity of categories, from indie consultants and developers to global integrators and agencies, in order to zero in on a couple of tiers, recognizing that at different phases of your program lifecycle you may need different types of support.

- The same agile-like approach that features an internal team following an iterative, adaptive, simulation-oriented process will make for better decisions.

- To the extent you want to develop internal expertise in customizing or extending the technology, look for firms that will work in co-development mode with your team.

- Don't get swayed by fancy or elaborate pitch meetings: what matters is how the firm really works, not what they say they can do, so focus your efforts on project simulations.

- Modify your evaluation criteria to reflect what the firm is delivering, and don't undervalue intangible considerations like communications and cultural fit.

- Compel the bidders to be transparent on hourly rates and their level of effort in a fine-grained way so that you can best align cost and business value.

Resources and Examples

This book cites several examples and templates. We've accumulated them all in one place where you can download and adapt them to your own needs.

You'll also find videos and tips to help coach you through some of the concepts in this book. Feel free to share those with colleagues to socialize the key tenets of adaptive technology selection. Also, please don't hesitate to provide feedback on these resources. Anything you'd change? Something useful to add? Let us know. Write to selectionbook@realstorygroup.com.

Find all the resources online at:
https://www.realstorygroup.com/SelectionBook

Sample Resources

- Video versions of chapter tips

- Example RFPs

- TCO spreadsheets

- Sample reference questions

- And more...

INDEX

in RFP, 96, 98–99

selecting/limiting, 43–45

specific roles, 41

structure of, 40–42

V

value creation, technology project justification, 4

vendors. *See also* suppliers

advice sources, 61–64

check box requirements sheets, 32

demos

canned demos, 104

demo-day cautions, 125–126

logistics of, 122–123, 125

RFD, 82, 87–88

role-specific break-out sessions, 123

selection team attendance, 123

session structure, 120–121

vendor cautions, 124

filtering

short list, 75–76

long list, 70–74

hot vendors, 78

incumbents as solutions, 60

influence on analyst reports, 63

large *vs.* small size, 74

PoC/bake-offs

post-PoC engagements, 150

questions generated by, 134–135

schedule for, 133–134

situations justifying bake-offs, 130–131

PSO (professional services organization), service firm types, 156–158

RFP responses, 98–99

vs. services firms, 64–67

W

workshops, information gathering process, 35–36

ACKNOWLEDGMENTS

Many people assisted with this book. Several colleagues at CMS Watch and Real Story Group helped build this methodology collaboratively over many years. Special thanks go to Apoorv Durga, Kashyap Kompella, Theresa Regli, Adriaan Bloem, Alan Pelz-Sharpe, Kas Thomas, and Matt Mullen. Ray Gingras and Lyza Morss assisted in the editorial and production process.

We also appreciate the input and support of the Rosenfeld Media team, including Marta Justak, Stephanie Zhong, and Lou Rosenfeld.

We are grateful to the many enterprise digital leaders who shared their projects and stories with us. Many were clients, more became friends.

And finally, this would not be possible without the constant support of our home teams. Carol and Lindsey, thanks for everything.

—Tony Byrne and Jarrod Gingras
June, 2017

ABOUT THE AUTHORS

 Tony Byrne is founder of Real Story Group (formerly CMS Watch), the only exclusively "buy-side" technology analyst firm in the world. Prior to that he was the head of software engineering and project management at a digital systems integrator, after working in journalism and international technical assistance.

Tony has a professional passion for helping large enterprises make sound strategic decisions that will set them up for long-term success. Across two decades he has advised several hundred organizations in dozens of countries around the globe in selecting the right technologies.

When not working, you can find Tony gardening, following the Green Bay Packers, playing with his dog, or traveling with his family.

• • •

 Jarrod Gingras is Real Story Group's Managing Director and an analyst covering digital workplace and marketing technologies. As a conference speaker and consultant, he regularly advises some of the world's largest and most complicated enterprises on their enterprise information challenges.

Prior to joining RSG, Jarrod worked as a web developer, information architect, and user interface designer at a systems integration firm, where he developed user-focused content management strategies and solutions for clients across many different industries.

Jarrod's passions include following Boston's sports teams, relaxing in Costa Rica with his wife Lindsey, and helping enterprises select the right technology for their unique needs.

Printed in the USA
CPSIA information can be obtained
at www.ICGtesting.com
JSHW011518221024
72172JS00007B/56